HMH SOCIAL STUDIES

Houghton
Mifflin
Harcourt

UNITED STATES HISTORY

BEGINNINGS TO 1877

Guided Reading Workbook

Printed in the U.S.A.

ISBN 978-0-544-66881-2

11 0928 24 23 22 21 20

4500790184 C D E F G

Contents

The Civil War

Reconstruction

HOW TO USE THIS BOOK

The *Guided Reading Workbook* was developed to help you master United States history content and build your reading and vocabulary skills. Review the next few pages to become familiar with the workbook's features and organization.

Lesson summary pages allow you to interact with the content and key terms and places from each lesson in a module. The summaries explain each lesson of your textbook in a way that is easy to understand.

Lesson numbers make it easy to find your place in the workbook.

The Main Ideas statements help focus your attention as you read the summaries.

Definitions for the lesson's Key Terms and People are listed before the Lesson Summary.

To help you find the content you need, headings in the Lesson Summary match those in your United States History book.

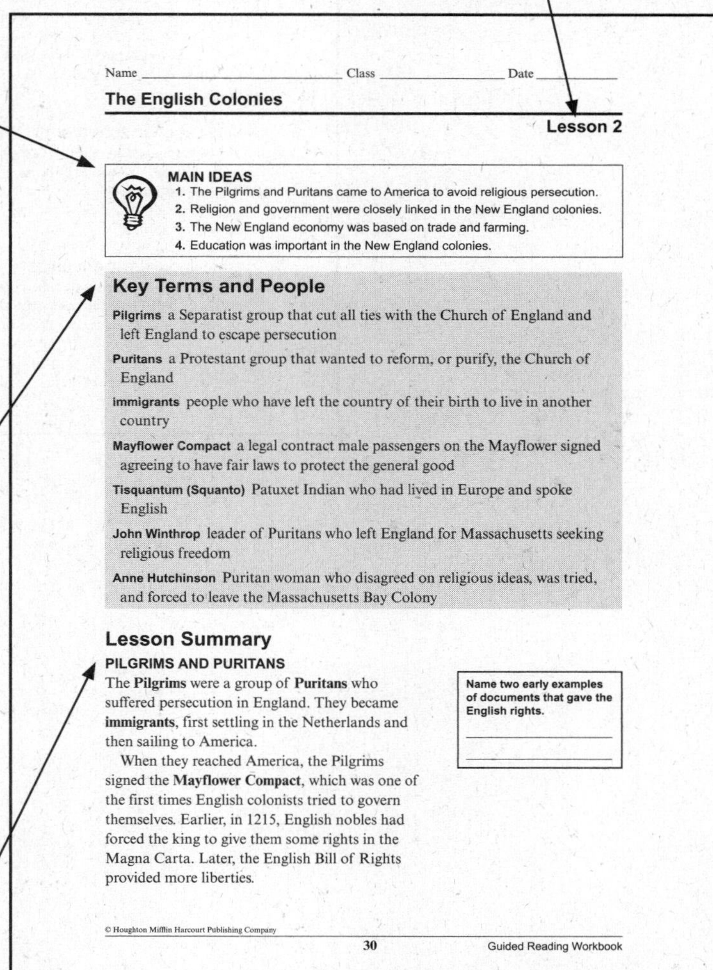

Name ______________ Class ______________ Date ______________

The English Colonies

Lesson 2

MAIN IDEAS
1. The Pilgrims and Puritans came to America to avoid religious persecution.
2. Religion and government were closely linked in the New England colonies.
3. The New England economy was based on trade and farming.
4. Education was important in the New England colonies.

Key Terms and People

Pilgrims a Separatist group that cut all ties with the Church of England and left England to escape persecution

Puritans a Protestant group that wanted to reform, or purify, the Church of England

immigrants people who have left the country of their birth to live in another country

Mayflower Compact a legal contract male passengers on the Mayflower signed agreeing to have fair laws to protect the general good

Tisquantum (Squanto) Patuxet Indian who had lived in Europe and spoke English

John Winthrop leader of Puritans who left England for Massachusetts seeking religious freedom

Anne Hutchinson Puritan woman who disagreed on religious ideas, was tried, and forced to leave the Massachusetts Bay Colony

Lesson Summary

PILGRIMS AND PURITANS

The **Pilgrims** were a group of **Puritans** who suffered persecution in England. They became **immigrants**, first settling in the Netherlands and then sailing to America.

When they reached America, the Pilgrims signed the **Mayflower Compact**, which was one of the first times English colonists tried to govern themselves. Earlier, in 1215, English nobles had forced the king to give them some rights in the Magna Carta. Later, the English Bill of Rights provided more liberties.

Name two early examples of documents that gave the English rights.

____

____

© Houghton Mifflin Harcourt Publishing Company

30 Guided Reading Workbook

Name ____________ Class ____________ Date ____________

Lesson 2, *continued*

The Pilgrims learned to fertilize their soil from **Tisquantum**. They invited him and 90 Wampanoag guests to a feast now known as Thanksgiving.

Religion and education played important parts in the Pilgrims' lives, which centered on families. Everyone worked hard, and women had rights that they did not have in England.

Puritans and merchants founded the Massachusetts Bay Colony. Tens of thousands of English men, women, and children would immigrate to it. **John Winthrop** led one group. Puritans believed they had a sacred agreement with God to build a Christian colony.

What was the Puritans' sacred agreement with God?

____

____

The lesson's key terms and people are in bold type to help you find them.

RELIGION AND GOVERNMENT IN NEW ENGLAND

Politics and religion were closely linked in Puritan New England. While some self-government existed, only chosen male church members could vote.

Some Puritans had different religious views from others. Minister Roger Williams supported the separation of the church from politics, so he was made to leave the colony. He founded Providence. **Anne Hutchinson** was also forced to leave the colony because of her ideas that differed from the group.

Underline the sentence that means women could not vote in Puritan New England.

NEW ENGLAND ECONOMY

The New England colonies had a hard climate and rocky soil, so the kind of farming done in Virginia was impossible there. Instead, they traded goods, fished, built ships, and became skilled craftspeople.

Compare sources of income in Virginia and New England.

____

____

____

EDUCATION IN THE COLONIES

New England parents wanted their children to read the Bible. They made laws requiring the education of children and set up town schools.

© Houghton Mifflin Harcourt Publishing Company 31 Guided Reading Workbook

As you read each summary, be sure to complete the questions and activities in the margin boxes. They help you check your reading comprehension and track important content.

Each lesson has at least one vocabulary activity that will help you to demonstrate your understanding of the key terms and people introduced in the lesson.

The Challenge Activity provides an opportunity for you to apply important critical thinking skills to information from the lesson summary.

Some vocabulary activities have a word bank. You can use it to help find answers or complete writing activities.

Various activities help you check your knowledge of key terms and people.

Writing activities require you to include key terms and people. Remember to check to make sure that you are using the terms and names correctly.

Name ______________________ Class ______________ Date __________

Lesson 2, *continued*

The colonists also founded Harvard College to teach ministers.

CHALLENGE ACTIVITY

Critical Thinking: Develop Develop three questions about the Pilgrims' contributions and research to answer them.

Anne Hutchinson	Mayflower Compact	Puritans
immigrants	Pilgrims	Tisquantum
John Winthrop		

DIRECTIONS Answer each question by writing a sentence that contains at least one word from the word bank.

1. Who was put on trial for his or her religious ideas and eventually forced out of the colony?

____

____

2. Who are people that leave their country of birth to live in another country?

____

____

3. Who showed the Pilgrims how to fertilize the soil on their farms and helped them establish relations with the chief of the local Wampanoag Indians?

____

____

4. Who led a group of Puritan colonists who left England for Massachusetts in search of religious freedom?

____

____

DIRECTIONS Choose at least five of the terms or names from the word bank. Use these words to write a letter that relates to the lesson.

© Houghton Mifflin Harcourt Publishing Company

32 Guided Reading Workbook

Lesson 1

MAIN IDEAS

1. Climate changes allowed Paleo-Indians to migrate to the Americas.
2. Major civilizations developed in Mesoamerica and South America.

Key Terms and People

environments climates and landscapes that surround living things

Bering Land Bridge a strip of land between Asia and present-day Alaska that was exposed by the lower sea levels of the Ice Age

Paleo-Indians people believed to have crossed the Bering Land Bridge

migration movement of people or animals from one region to another

hunter-gatherers people who obtain food by hunting animals and gathering wild plants

culture a group's set of common values and traditions

Lesson Summary

EARLY MIGRATIONS TO THE AMERICAS

Many scientists believe that the first people arrived in North America during the last Ice Age. At that time the **environment** changed. Large amounts of water froze, forming glaciers. Water levels in the oceans dropped to more than 300 feet lower than they are today. A strip of land called the **Bering Land Bridge** was exposed between Asia and Alaska.

How did the formation of glaciers during the Ice Age allow for migration to North America?

____

____

____

No one knows exactly when or how people crossed into North America. There is evidence that people called **Paleo-Indians** crossed the bridge to Alaska between 38,000 and 10,000 BC. The **migration** took place over a long time. The descendants of the migrants went as far as the southern tip of South America. These people were **hunter-gatherers**. They hunted animals and gathered wild plants for food. Different environments influenced the development of different Native American societies.

Does evidence tell exactly when the Paleo-Indians crossed into North America? Explain.

____

____

____

EARLY MESOAMERICAN AND SOUTH AMERICAN SOCIETIES

Some of the earliest American **cultures** arose in Mesoamerica. This is a region that includes the southern part of what is now Mexico and northern Central America. The Olmec developed the earliest known civilization in Mesoamerica around 1200 BC. The Olmec are known for their stone buildings and sculptures. By 400 BC, when their civilization ended, trade had spread Olmec culture.

Underline the sentence that tells when the first civilization developed in Mesoamerica.

The Maya civilization followed the Olmec. The Maya built large stone temples and pyramids. They built canals that controlled the flow of water through their cities. The Maya civilization began to collapse in the 900s, but historians are still not sure why.

What evidence do we have that cultures existed in Mesoamerica before the Aztecs?

____

____

____

The Aztec were fierce warriors. They migrated to south and central Mexico in the mid-1100s. They conquered many towns, built a large empire, and controlled a huge trading network. The Aztec capital, Tenochtitlán (tay-nawch-teet-LAHN), founded in 1325, became the greatest city in the Americas and one of the world's largest cities. The Aztec became rich on trade and tributes paid by conquered people.

What was the greatest city in the Americas during the height of the Aztec culture?

____

The Inca began as a small tribe in the Andes Mountains. In the mid-1400s, the Inca began expanding their empire until it included much of the western coast of South America and had more than 12 million people. The Inca people had a strong central government. They built a network of roads and bridges that connected all parts of the territory.

CHALLENGE ACTIVITY

Critical Thinking: Evaluate Imagine that you lived in Mesoamerica or South America before the arrival of Europeans. Write a short paragraph describing which of the four civilizations discussed above you would have preferred to live in. Be sure to support your answer.

Bering Land Bridge	environment	migration
culture	hunter-gatherers	Paleo-Indians

DIRECTIONS On the line provided before each statement, write **T** if a statement is true or **F** if a statement is false. If the statement is false, find a word or phrase in the word bank that makes the statement true and write it on the line below the statement.

______ 1. Culture is the movement of people or animals from one region to another.

____

______ 2. Migration is the climate and landscape that surround living things.

____

______ 3. Paleo-Indians crossed the Bering Land Bridge into Alaska between 38,000 and 10,000 BC.

____

______ 4. A group's set of common values and traditions is called a Bering Land Bridge.

____

______ 5. Paleo-Indians were hunter-gatherers who lived by hunting animals and gathering wild plants.

____

______ 6. The culture was a strip of solid land believed to have once connected Asia and present-day Alaska.

____

Name ______________________________ Class ____________________ Date ____________

America, Africa, and Europe before 1500

Lesson 2

MAIN IDEAS

1. Several early societies developed in North America long before Europeans explored the continent.
2. Geographic areas influenced Native American cultures.
3. Despite their differences, Native American cultures shared similar beliefs and practices.

Key Terms and People

pueblos aboveground houses made of a heavy clay called adobe

kivas underground ceremonial chambers at the center of each Anasazi community

totems ancestor or animal spirits of the Native Americans of the Pacific Northwest

teepees cone-shaped shelters made of animal hides by the nomadic plains people

matrilineal tracing a society's ancestry through mothers

Iroquois League an alliance of Native Americans in northeastern North America

Lesson Summary

EARLY SOCIETIES

The earliest people in North America were hunter-gatherers. By 1500 BC people in the southwestern part of North America had farm cultures and grew maize. The Anasazi (an-nuh-SAH-zee) used irrigation to increase food production in the dry climate. They lived in pit houses dug into the ground. Later they built **pueblos**. The Anasazi often built complex houses on cliff walls to defend against attacks. They also built **kivas**, sacred areas at the center of the community.

The Anasazi began abandoning their villages after living in them for hundreds of years. Drought, disease, or raids by other tribes may have caused this move.

How would building on cliff walls provide protection for the Anasazi?

____

____

____

Why would drought be one of the possible reasons that the Anasazi moved from their homes?

____

____

____

After 1000 BC several farming societies developed in the eastern part of North America. They built large burial mounds to honor their dead. More than 10,000 mounds have been found in the Ohio River valley alone. The mound-building cultures declined and no longer existed by the early 1700s.

NATIVE AMERICAN CULTURE AREAS

The culture of Native American people varied depending on geography. In the far north, in present-day Alaska and Canada, Native Americans survived primarily by hunting and fishing, living in small groups. Farther south, along the Pacific Northwest, larger groups thrived on the abundant wildlife. They carved tall poles with **totems**—symbols of animal or ancestor spirits. These had religious and cultural meaning.

What was the significance of the characters carved on totem poles?

____

____

____

Farther south along the Pacific and the Sierra Nevada Mountains, people fished, hunted, gathered plants, and lived in small groups of families. In the drier areas of the Southwest, Pueblo groups had to develop agriculture to adapt to the climate. They lived in towns of up to 1,000 people. Others, such as the Apache and Navajo, formed nomadic groups that survived by hunting, foraging, or raiding other villages.

Most Native Americans of the Great Plains were nomadic hunters. They survived on the abundant wildlife of the grasslands, living in **teepees** made of animal hides. Some Plains groups were farmers, including the Pawnee, who had a **matrilineal** society. In the east, many Native Americans had small villages and lived by farming, hunting, and fishing. The **Iroquois League** was an alliance of many groups that defended one another.

Describe the food and shelter of the Native Americans of the Great Plains.

____

____

____

NATIVE AMERICAN LANGUAGES

Language played an important part in the cultural diversity of Native Americans 1,000 years ago. About 300 different languages were spoken. Those languages developed from 29 original languages.

Underline the sentence that tells how many different languages were spoken by Native Americans.

SIMILAR BELIEFS AND PRACTICES

Although they had many different cultures, Native Americans shared certain beliefs. Their religions were linked to nature, and they believed that the land was for the use of everyone.

What beliefs did Native Americans share?

____

____

____

CHALLENGE ACTIVITY

Critical Thinking: Compare Pick two Native American groups from two different culture areas. Make a chart comparing these two societies.

DIRECTIONS Write two adjectives or descriptive phrases that describe each term.

1. Iroquois League ______________________________
2. kivas ______________________________
3. matrilineal ______________________________

   ____
4. pueblos ______________________________
5. teepees ______________________________
6. totems ______________________________

DIRECTIONS Read each sentence and fill in the blank with the word in the word pair that best completes the sentence.

7. ____________________ are cone-shaped shelters. (Kivas/Teepees)
8. Pawnee society was ____________________, which means that people traced their ancestry through their mothers, not their fathers. (matrilineal/totems)
9. The Anasazi dug pit houses and later built ____________________, or aboveground houses made of heavy clay called adobe. (pueblos/kivas)
10. Native Americans in the Pacific Northwest carved images of ancestor or animal spirits called ____________________ on tall, wooden poles. (totems/teepees)

Name ______________________________ Class ____________________ Date__________

Lesson 3

MAIN IDEAS

1. The Empire of Ghana was the first of three great West African trading kingdoms.
2. Like Ghana, the empires of Mali and Songhai grew strong by controlling trade.

Key Terms and People

Berbers North African people who established trade routes through West Africa

Mansa Musa a Muslim king who ruled the Mali Empire at the height of its power and who spread Islamic influence through a large part of West Africa

hajj in Islam, a pilgrimage to the holy city of Mecca

Askia the Great the Muslim ruler who led Songhai to the height of its power

mosques Islamic places of worship

Lesson Summary

WEST AFRICA'S GREAT KINGDOMS

West African trade routes were originally controlled by the **Berbers**, a people of North Africa. Later, three great kingdoms developed in West Africa by winning control of these trade routes.

What was the main source of the wealth and power of all the West African empires?

____

____

Ghana (GAH-nuh) formed when farmers banded together to protect themselves from herders. They built armies whose superior iron weapons let them take control of the trade in salt and gold. Ghana raised money by forcing traders who passed through its lands to pay taxes. The trade routes brought Ghana into contact with different cultures and beliefs. In the 1060s a Muslim group attacked Ghana. They forced its leaders to convert to Islam. Although Ghana was weakened and eventually fell, the influence of Islam remained strong.

What river flowed through both Ghana and Mali?

____

____

Like Ghana, Mali (MAH-lee) was located along the upper Niger River. The fertile soil and the control of trade on the river allowed Mali to become rich and powerful. Its most famous ruler was a Muslim king, **Mansa Musa** (MAHN-sah moos-SAH). Under his leadership Mali grew in wealth and power. Traders came to Timbuktu (tim-buhk-TOO), an important city, to trade for salt, gold, metals, shells, and other goods.

Because he was a devout Muslim, Mansa Musa went on a **hajj**, or a pilgrimage to Mecca. His influence helped bring Islam to a large part of West Africa. In the 1300s Mansa Musa conquered a kingdom called Songhai (SAWNG-hy). These people also lived along the Niger River. As the Mali kingdom weakened in the 1400s, Songhai regained independence.

One of the greatest Songhai rulers was Muhammad Ture. He chose a military title, *askia*, and became known as **Askia the Great**. Like Mansa Musa, Askia was a devout Muslim who supported education and learning. His cities had great **mosques**, schools, and libraries. He built a professional army and organized Songhai with governors who were loyal to him. Songhai declined soon after Askia the Great lost power.

What did Mansa Musa and Askia the Great have in common?

____

____

CHALLENGE ACTIVITY

Critical Thinking: Elaborate Imagine that you live in one of the kingdoms discussed in this section. Write a brief description of what an average day might be like.

Askia the Great	hajj	mosques
Berbers	Mansa Musa	

DIRECTIONS On the line provided before each statement, write **T** if a statement is true or **F** if a statement is false. If the statement is false, find a word or phrase in the word bank that makes the statement true. Write the new sentence on the lines provided.

______ 1. For hundreds of years, West Africans did not profit much from the Saharan trade because the routes were controlled by <u>mosques</u>.

____

____

______ 2. Mali reached the height of its wealth, power, and fame under <u>Askia the Great</u>.

____

____

______ 3. With religion being very important to Mansa Musa, he left Mali in 1324 on a <u>hajj</u>.

____

____

______ 4. Mansa Musa began building <u>mosques</u>, which were used for Muslim prayer.

____

____

______ 5. <u>Askia the Great</u> supported education and learning and created an effective government.

____

____

Name ______________________ Class ______________ Date __________

Lesson 4

MAIN IDEAS

1. The Greeks and Romans established new forms of government.
2. During the Middle Ages, society eventually changed from a feudal system to a system with a middle class of artisans and merchants.
3. The Renaissance was a time of rebirth in the arts and in learning.

Key Terms and People

Socrates Greek teacher who wanted people to question their own beliefs

Plato Greek philosopher who wrote *The Republic*, about an ideal society

Aristotle Greek philosopher who thought people should live based on reason

reason clear and ordered thinking

democracy a form of government in which people rule themselves

knights feudal warriors who fought on horseback

Black Death a disease that spread across Europe, killing 25 million people

Michelangelo Italian Renaissance artist known for paintings and sculpture

Leonardo da Vinci Italian artist, inventor, engineer, and mapmaker of the Renaissance

Johannes Gutenberg German inventor of the moveable type printing press

joint-stock companies businesses in which a group of people invest together

Lesson Summary

GREEK AND ROMAN INFLUENCES

Ancient Greeks valued human reason. They believed in the power of the human mind to think, explain, and understand life. Three of the greatest Greek thinkers were **Socrates**, **Plato**, and **Aristotle**. All three were philosophers and teachers. Aristotle taught that people should live lives based on **reason**, or clear and ordered thinking.

Who were three of the greatest Greek thinkers?

____

____

One of the most lasting contributions of the Greeks is the political system they established during the Classical Period. A **democracy** is a government in which people rule themselves. Rome later formed a type of democracy called a

Underline the sentence that describes the political system that the Greeks contributed.

republic. In a republic, people elect representatives to rule them. These political ideas still influence world governments, including that of the United States.

MIDDLE AGES

After the fall of the Roman Empire, Europe was divided into many small kingdoms. A system called feudalism was established in which nobles gave **knights** land. In exchange, the knights protected the nobles.

In the 1000s important changes began to occur in Europe. The Crusades brought trade with places outside Europe. Trade also introduced new products and ideas. It also brought a disease known as the **Black Death**. So many people died that there was a shortage of workers. A new middle class made up of artisans and merchants developed. Cities became important as commercial centers for trade.

How did the Black Death cause changes in commerce?

____

____

____

RENAISSANCE

A key feature of the Renaissance was a love of art and education. During the Renaissance the focus of learning and art shifted from religion to people. Two of the great Renaissance artists, **Michelangelo** and **Leonardo da Vinci**, are famous for their paintings, sculpture, and architecture. Their art reflected the value of the human being. The printing press developed by **Johannes Gutenberg** (GOOT-uhn-berk) helped spread new ideas in science, math, and literature.

Increased trade caused a commercial revolution. Italian cities became important trading centers. As commerce grew, so did the need for banks. Merchants created **joint-stock companies** in which groups of people invested together.

Underline a key feature of the Renaissance.

What helped spread new ideas during the Renaissance?

____

____

____

CHALLENGE ACTIVITY

Critical Thinking: Make Inferences How did new ideas and trade change people's lives in Europe? For each of the time periods discussed, name one thing you think would have changed for the people living at the time.

DIRECTIONS Look at each set of four vocabulary terms following each number. On the line provided, write the letter of the term that does not relate to the other terms.

______ 1. a. Socrates
b. Aristotle
c. knights
d. Plato

______ 2. a. Black Death
b. Leonardo da Vinci
c. joint-stock companies
d. Johannes Gutenberg

DIRECTIONS Read each sentence and fill in the blank with the word in the word pair that best completes the sentence.

3. ____________________ wrote a work called *The Republic*. (Aristotle/Plato)

4. The form of government in which people rule themselves is called ______________________. (reason/democracy)

5. Aristotle taught ____________________, or clear and ordered thinking, as a basis on which people should live their lives. (classical/reason)

6. Europe's economy declined dramatically after the ______________________ killed an estimated 25 million people. (knights/Black Death)

7. After ____________________ invented the printing press, thousands of people began reading the same books. (Johannes Gutenberg /Socrates)

Name ______________________ Class ______________ Date __________

Lesson 1

MAIN IDEAS

1. Vikings were skilled sailors, and they were the first Europeans to reach North America.
2. Prince Henry the Navigator established a school for sailors and provided financial support that enabled the Portuguese to start exploring the oceans.
3. Portuguese sailors sailed around Africa and found a sea route to Asia.

Key Terms and People

Leif Eriksson Viking who landed in present-day Canada in the year 1000

Henry the Navigator Portuguese prince who established a school of navigation and paid for expeditions

astrolabe device used to determine location based on the position of the stars

caravels Portuguese ships that used triangular sails to sail against the wind

Lesson Summary

VIKING SAILORS REACH NORTH AMERICA

The Vikings were the first Europeans to make contact with North America. They were skilled sailors who developed a new style of ship, the longship. It was more stable on rough seas.

In the year 1000 **Leif Eriksson**, the son of Erik the Red, set off for Greenland. Strong winds blew his ship off course. So he landed on the North American coast. The Vikings settled in a coastal area that Eriksson called Vinland. However, they left after a few years. Europeans did not return to the continent for centuries.

Who were the first Europeans to settle in North America?

____

LOOKING TOWARD THE SEA

In the early 1400s Portugal became a leader in world exploration. Although he never set out on a voyage himself, Prince **Henry the Navigator** helped Portugal's explorers succeed. He built an observatory and a school of navigation to teach better methods of sailing. Europeans had several reasons to explore the world. They wanted spices from Asia, and they wanted to learn more about

What European country led world exploration in the early 1400s?

____

Asia and its culture. They also wanted to convert Asians to the Christian faith.

European sailors were able to travel in open seas without landmarks to guide them because of better maps and new technology. Sailors used the magnetic compass for directions. The **astrolabe** was used to chart a ship's location based on the position of the stars. The **caravel** was a new kind of ship that was smaller, lighter, and easier to steer than heavy galleons that had been used before. Caravels used triangular sails that allowed ships to sail against the wind and rudders that improved steering.

Why did Europeans want to explore the world?

____

____

____

How did new technology benefit Portuguese exploration?

____

____

____

A SEA ROUTE TO ASIA

In the 1400s Portuguese sailors traveled south along the coast of Africa, setting up trading posts along the way. In 1497 a Portuguese expedition led by Vasco da Gama sailed around the southern tip of Africa and reached India. These successful voyages had a number of effects, both positive and negative. Portugal's wealth and power increased. However, these travels eventually led to the spread of the slave trade. Other European nations soon began looking for their own sea routes to Asia.

What was the first sea route from Europe to Asia?

____

____

CHALLENGE ACTIVITY

Critical Thinking: Make Inferences The Portuguese had laws that included severe penalties for letting sailors from other countries see the maps the Portuguese created from their expeditions. Write a paragraph explaining why they wanted to keep these maps secret.

DIRECTIONS Look at each set of terms below. On the line provided, write the letter of the term that does not relate to the others.

_____ 1. a. Portuguese
b. smaller, lighter, and easier-to-steer ships
c. Vikings
d. caravels

_____ 2. a. astrolabe
b. new type of ship
c. ship's location
d. charted the position of the stars

_____ 3. a. Leif Eriksson
b. caravel
c. Henry the Navigator
d. exploration

_____ 4. a. Portugal
b. Prince Henry the Navigator
c. observatory
d. Viking

_____ 5. a. magnetic compass
b. Leif Eriksson
c. Vikings
d. Erik the Red

_____ 6. a. longships
b. Vasco da Gama
c. caravels
d. galleons

Name ______________________ Class ______________ Date __________

MAIN IDEAS

1. Christopher Columbus sailed across the Atlantic Ocean and reached a continent that was previously unknown to him.
2. After Columbus's voyages, other explorers sailed to the Americas.

Key Terms and People

Christopher Columbus sailor from Genoa, Italy

Line of Demarcation imaginary boundary in the Atlantic dividing Spanish and Portuguese territories

Treaty of Tordesillas agreement between Spain and Portugal moving the Line of Demarcation

Ferdinand Magellan Portuguese navigator whose expedition circumnavigated the globe

circumnavigate to go all the way around

Columbian Exchange the transfer of plants and animals between the Americas and Asia, Africa, and Europe

Lesson Summary

COLUMBUS SAILS ACROSS THE ATLANTIC

Christopher Columbus, a sailor from Genoa, Italy, believed that he could reach Asia by sailing west across the Atlantic Ocean. He asked King Ferdinand and Queen Isabella of Spain to pay for an expedition. In return, he promised great riches, new territory, and Catholic converts.

Sailing with three ships, Columbus reached an island in the Bahamas in 1492. Columbus thought he had found a new route to Asia. In reality, he had reached another continent that was unknown to him. Columbus made three more journeys to the Americas during his lifetime. When he died in 1506, he still believed that he had reached Asia.

The voyages of Columbus changed the way Europeans saw the world. It also created conflict between European nations. In 1493 the pope

Why did the Spanish and other Europeans want to find a route to Asia?

____

____

Underline the sentence that explains where Columbus thought he had landed.

issued a decree that created the **Line of Demarcation**. This imaginary boundary divided the Atlantic Ocean between Spain and Portugal. The Portuguese king believed the arrangement favored Spain. So the leaders of the two nations signed the **Treaty of Tordesillas**. This treaty moved the Line of Demarcation 800 miles west and prevented a war between the two countries.

What was the result of the Treaty of Tordesillas?

____

____

OTHER EXPLORERS SAIL TO THE AMERICAS

After Columbus, other explorers sailed across the Atlantic Ocean. In 1501 Amerigo Vespucci became convinced that he had not reached Asia. He thought he had discovered a "new world." A German mapmaker labeled the continents across the ocean as America in Vespucci's honor.

Vasco Núñez de Balboa, a Spanish explorer, crossed the jungles of Central America to see the Pacific Ocean in 1513. In 1519 Portuguese navigator **Ferdinand Magellan** sailed around the southern tip of South America and into the Pacific. Magellan was killed in the Philippine Islands. However, one ship from his expedition was the first to **circumnavigate** the globe.

Why do people say that Ferdinand Magellan circumnavigated the globe even though he died on the way?

____

____

European explorers and settlers took plants, animals, and other things such as diseases with them to America. They brought back American plants, animals, and diseases, too. This transfer was called the **Columbian Exchange** because it started with the explorations of Columbus. Over time a trading pattern developed. It involved the exchange of raw materials, manufactured products, and slaves among Europe, Africa, and the Americas.

CHALLENGE ACTIVITY

Critical Thinking: Elaborate Imagine you are a sailor on one of Columbus's ships. Write a short poem about the first sighting of land in the present-day Bahamas.

Atlantic Ocean	diseases	Pacific Ocean
Christopher Columbus	Ferdinand Magellan	Queen Isabella I
circumnavigate	King Ferdinand	Treaty of Tordesillas
Columbian Exchange	Line of Demarcation	

DIRECTIONS Choose five of the terms or people from the word bank. Use the words to write an email message to your friend explaining what you learned in the lesson.

____

____

____

____

____

____

____

____

____

____

____

____

____

Name ______________________ Class ______________ Date ____________

New Empires in the Americas

Lesson 3

MAIN IDEAS

1. Spanish conquistadors conquered the Aztec and Inca empires.
2. Spanish explorers traveled through the borderlands of New Spain, claiming more land.
3. Spanish settlers treated Native Americans harshly, forcing them to work on plantations and in mines.

Key Terms and People

conquistadors Spanish soldiers who led military expeditions in the Americas

Hernán Cortés conquistador who conquered the Aztec empire

Moctezuma II ruler of the Aztec empire during the early 1500s

Francisco Pizarro conquistador who captured the Inca capital and killed the Inca leaders

encomienda system system that gave settlers the right to tax Native Americans or to make them work

plantations large farms that grew just one kind of crop and made huge profits for their owners

Bartolomé de Las Casas priest who wanted to convert Native Americans to Christianity by treating them in a better manner

Lesson Summary

SPANISH CONQUISTADORS

The Spanish sent **conquistadors** to the Americas on military expeditions. Conquistador **Hernán Cortés** went to present-day Mexico in 1519. He had heard of land to the west ruled by **Moctezuma II**, the king of the Aztec empire. The Spaniards believed the Aztec lands were a rich source of gold and silver. They also wanted to convert the Aztec to Christianity.

Why might Cortés have wanted to conquer the Aztec?

____

____

The conquistadors were greatly outnumbered. However, they had superior weapons and formed alliances with enemies of the Aztec. Cortés took control of the Aztec capital and killed Moctezuma. Smallpox and other European diseases sped up the fall of the Aztec empire.

What advantage did the Spanish have over the Aztec?

____

____

While seeking gold, **Francisco Pizarro** led his troops to capture the great Inca capital at Cuzco. Within a few years, Pizarro had conquered the entire Inca empire. The Spanish then began to create a vast empire. They called it New Spain. They established settlements to serve as trading posts, missions to convert local Native Americans to Catholicism, and military bases.

Why did Pizarro first enter the Inca empire?

____

____

____

EXPLORING THE BORDERLANDS OF NEW SPAIN

Spain's empire in America extended well beyond the lands taken from the Aztec and Inca. Regions claimed by the Spanish explorers included the island of Puerto Rico, the coast of present-day Florida, and the coastal regions of the Gulf of Mexico. The Spanish also explored what is now the southwestern United States. They were looking for cities of gold that were rumored to exist there. They traveled through unclaimed areas of Texas, Oklahoma, and as far north as Kansas.

SPANISH TREATMENT OF NATIVE AMERICANS

California was among the last borderlands settled by the Spanish. To pay back settlers for their work, Spain established the **encomienda system**. It gave settlers the right to tax Native Americans and make them work. Most of the workers were treated as slaves. They were forced to work on **plantations** in New Spain. Many Native Americans died of disease and exhaustion. The priest **Bartolomé de Las Casas** spoke out against the encomienda system.

Why might de Las Casas have spoken out against the encomienda system?

____

____

____

CHALLENGE ACTIVITY

Critical Thinking: Identify Cause and Effect Make a chart showing the causes and effects of Spain's conquests in the Americas.

Bartolomé de Las Casas	Francisco Pizarro	Moctezuma II
conquistadors	Hernán Cortés	plantations
encomienda system		

DIRECTIONS Answer each question by writing a sentence that contains a word from the word bank.

1. Which priest wanted to convert Native Americans to Christianity?

____

____

2. What were the farms the Spanish operated in the Americas called?

____

____

3. What Spanish system gave settlers the right to tax local Native Americans?

____

____

4. Which conquistador defeated the Inca?

____

____

5. Who was the king of the Aztec empire when the conquistadors arrived in Mexico?

____

____

6. Who was the conquistador that conquered the Aztec empire?

____

____

7. What were the Spanish soldiers who conquered the Americas called?

____

____

Name ______________________ Class ________________ Date __________

Lesson 4

MAIN IDEAS

1. Events in Europe affected settlement of North America.
2. Several explorers searched for a Northwest Passage to the Pacific Ocean.
3. European nations raced to establish empires in North America.

Key Terms and People

Protestant Reformation religious movement that began as an effort to reform the Catholic Church

Protestants reformers who protested some of the Catholic Church's practices

Spanish Armada huge fleet of Spanish warships

Northwest Passage water route through North America that would allow ships to sail from the Atlantic to the Pacific

Jacques Cartier French explorer who sailed up the Saint Lawrence River looking for the Northwest Passage

charter document giving permission to start a colony

Lesson Summary

EVENTS IN EUROPE

In 1517 a priest named Martin Luther launched the **Protestant Reformation**. His followers were called **Protestants**. Luther said the Catholic Church was too rich and abused its powers. The printing press helped spread Protestant ideas because large numbers of Bibles could be printed. More people could read the Bible on their own instead of depending on priests to explain it.

How did the printing press help spread Protestant ideas?

____

____

____

Often conflicts between Catholics and Protestants led to war. In the late 1500s French Catholics fought French Protestants known as Huguenots. Many Huguenots traveled to the Americas for religious freedom. In 1534 King Henry VIII established the Church of England, or Anglican Church. Henry declared himself head of this Protestant Church. By breaking with the Catholic Church, King Henry made himself

What were French Protestants called?

____

the enemy of other European rulers who were Catholic.

King Philip II of Spain, a Catholic ruler, put together a large fleet called the **Spanish Armada**. He wanted to defeat the Protestant nation of England. England had fewer ships, but they were quick. In July 1588 the English navy defeated the Armada. The defeat hurt the Spanish, whose economy was in trouble because of inflation. Inflation is a rise in prices caused by an increase in the amount of money in use.

What helped England's navy defeat the Spanish Armada?

____

____

SEARCH FOR A NORTHWEST PASSAGE

European nations wanted to find a **Northwest Passage** in North America that would allow ships to sail from the Atlantic to the Pacific, providing a shortcut to Asia. Early searches explored the coast from Canada to North Carolina. **Jacques Cartier** explored the Saint Lawrence River and claimed lands for France. The Northwest Passage was not found. However, the voyages led to more interest in North America.

EUROPEAN PRESENCE IN NORTH AMERICA

Spain and Portugal claimed much of South and Central America but left most of North America unexplored. In the late 1500s Sir Walter Raleigh of England received a **charter** to found a colony in present-day Virginia. The first colonists did not stay, but Raleigh sent more colonists. Those colonists disappeared.

France built settlements in Florida, but the Spanish soon drove them out. In the 1600s French colonies were established on the Saint Lawrence River. The French claimed lands extending to the Mississippi River. The Dutch founded the town of New Amsterdam on Manhattan Island. Swedish settlers started New Sweden along the Delaware River, but it was conquered by the Dutch colonists in 1655.

What happened to French settlers in Florida?

____

____

CHALLENGE ACTIVITY

Critical Thinking: Summarize Write a bulleted list summarizing the early settlements of the Americas.

DIRECTIONS Write two adjectives or descriptive phrases that describe the term, person, or event.

1. charter ____

____

2. Jacques Cartier ____

____

3. Northwest Passage ____

____

4. Protestant Reformation ____

____

5. Protestants ____

____

6. Spanish Armada ____

____

DIRECTIONS Read each sentence and fill in the blank with the word in the word pair that best completes the sentence.

7. ________________________, a French explorer, led a major French exploration of what is now Canada and claimed lands for France. (Jacques Cartier/Sir Walter Raleigh)
8. The ________________________ were reformers who protested some of the Catholic Church's practices. (Spanish Armada/Protestants)
9. A ________________________ is a document giving permission to start a colony. (Reformation/charter)
10. Europeans wanted to find a ________________________, a water route through North America that would provide a shortcut to Asia. (Northwest Passage/Spanish Armada)

Name ______________________________ Class __________________ Date ____________

The English Colonies

Lesson 1

MAIN IDEAS

1. Jamestown was the first permanent English settlement in America.
2. Daily life in Virginia was challenging to the colonists.
3. Religious freedom and economic opportunities were motives for founding other southern colonies, including Maryland, the Carolinas, and Georgia.
4. Farming and slavery were important to the economies of the southern colonies.

Key Terms and People

Jamestown an English settlement in Virginia founded in 1607

John Smith a colonist and leader of Jamestown

Pocahontas a Powhatan Indian who married Jamestown colonist John Rolfe

indentured servants colonists who reached America by working for free for other people who had paid for their journeys

Bacon's Rebellion an uprising led by Nathaniel Bacon against high taxes

Toleration Act of 1649 an act that made limiting the religious rights of Christians a crime

Olaudah Equiano a former slave who wrote down his experiences

slave codes laws to control slaves

Lesson Summary

SETTLEMENT IN JAMESTOWN

Life in **Jamestown** was hard because few colonists knew how to grow crops. Captain **John Smith** worried about the lack of food, and many colonists starved. The Powhatan helped them grow crops.

Why did many colonists in Jamestown starve?

____

____

Pocahontas helped unite the Powhatan and the colonists, but she died in 1617. Fighting broke out between the colonists and the Powhatan and went on for the next 20 years. The colony existed under the authority of a governor chosen by the king.

DAILY LIFE IN VIRGINIA

Colonists began forming large farms called plantations where they grew tobacco. At first **indentured servants** worked on plantations. The demand for workers became greater than the number of indentured servants. So in 1619 the first Africans came to Virginia. The cost for slaves was not very high. These factors led wealthy farmers to begin using slave labor.

Colonial officials began raising taxes and encouraging trade with Native Americans. In 1676 Nathaniel Bacon, a wealthy frontier farmer, led **Bacon's Rebellion**. Bacon and his followers did not agree with leaders, so they burned Jamestown.

What happened to Jamestown in 1676?

____

____

OTHER SOUTHERN COLONIES

Maryland was founded south of Virginia as a new colony for Catholics. In the 1640s Protestants began moving in, which led to religious problems between Protestants and Catholics. The **Toleration Act of 1649** made limiting religious rights of Christians a crime in Maryland.

The Carolinas and Georgia were formed south of Virginia and Maryland. South Carolina had many large plantations, and owners bought slaves to work on them. In Georgia many huge rice plantations were worked by thousands of slaves.

Underline the sentence that describes the purpose of the Toleration Act of 1649.

ECONOMIES OF THE SOUTHERN COLONIES

The economies of the southern colonies were based on farming. Many small farms and some small plantations meant a large group of workers was needed, so African slaves became these workers. Slavery was brutal. A man named **Olaudah Equiano**, who had been enslaved, wrote that slaves were often tortured, murdered, and treated with great cruelty. Most of the southern states passed **slave codes** to control slaves.

How did a former slave describe treatment of slaves?

____

____

____

CHALLENGE ACTIVITY

Critical Thinking: Sequence Create a timeline showing the dates of important events in the southern colonies.

Bacon's Rebellion	indentured servants	Pocahontas
Jamestown	Olaudah Equiano	Toleration Act of 1649
John Smith		

DIRECTIONS Read each sentence and choose the correct term from the word bank to replace the underlined term. Write the term in the space provided and then define the term in your own words.

1. <u>John Rolfe</u> wrote about the brutal conditions he experienced as a slave.

 ____

 Your definition: ______________________________

 ____

 ____

2. Colonists called <u>Pilgrims</u> signed contracts agreeing to work on plantations and farms in exchange for the payment of their journey to America. ______________________________

 Your definition: ______________________________

 ____

 ____

3. A group of former indentured servants led by a wealthy frontier farmer began an uprising called the slave codes. ______________________________

   Your definition: ______________________________

   ____

   ____

4. The plantation system made restricting religious rights of Christians a crime, and was the first law supporting religious tolerance passed in the English colonies. ______________________________

   Your definition: ______________________________

   ____

   ____

Name ______________________ Class ______________ Date __________

The English Colonies

Lesson 2

MAIN IDEAS

1. The Pilgrims and Puritans came to America to avoid religious persecution.
2. Religion and government were closely linked in the New England colonies.
3. The New England economy was based on trade and farming.
4. Education was important in the New England colonies.

Key Terms and People

Pilgrims a Separatist group that cut all ties with the Church of England and left England to escape persecution

Puritans a Protestant group that wanted to reform, or purify, the Church of England

immigrants people who have left the country of their birth to live in another country

Mayflower Compact a legal contract male passengers on the Mayflower signed agreeing to have fair laws to protect the general good

Tisquantum (Squanto) Patuxet Indian who had lived in Europe and spoke English

John Winthrop leader of Puritans who left England for Massachusetts seeking religious freedom

Anne Hutchinson Puritan woman who disagreed on religious ideas, was tried, and forced to leave the Massachusetts Bay Colony

Lesson Summary

PILGRIMS AND PURITANS

The **Pilgrims** were a group of **Puritans** who suffered persecution in England. They became **immigrants**, first settling in the Netherlands and then sailing to America.

When they reached America, the Pilgrims signed the **Mayflower Compact**, which was one of the first times English colonists tried to govern themselves. Earlier, in 1215, English nobles had forced the king to give them some rights in the Magna Carta. Later, the English Bill of Rights provided more liberties.

Name two early examples of documents that gave the English rights.

____

____

The Pilgrims learned to fertilize their soil from **Tisquantum**. They invited him and 90 Wampanoag guests to a feast now known as Thanksgiving.

Religion and education played important parts in the Pilgrims' lives, which centered on families. Everyone worked hard, and women had rights that they did not have in England.

Puritans and merchants founded the Massachusetts Bay Colony. Tens of thousands of English men, women, and children would immigrate to it. **John Winthrop** led one group. Puritans believed they had a sacred agreement with God to build a Christian colony.

What was the Puritans' sacred agreement with God?

____

____

RELIGION AND GOVERNMENT IN NEW ENGLAND

Politics and religion were closely linked in Puritan New England. While some self-government existed, only chosen male church members could vote.

Underline the sentence that means women could not vote in Puritan New England.

Some Puritans had different religious views from others. Minister Roger Williams supported the separation of the church from politics, so he was made to leave the colony. He founded Providence. **Anne Hutchinson** was also forced to leave the colony because of her ideas that differed from the group.

NEW ENGLAND ECONOMY

The New England colonies had a hard climate and rocky soil, so the kind of farming done in Virginia was impossible there. Instead, they traded goods, fished, built ships, and became skilled craftspeople.

Compare sources of income in Virginia and New England.

____

____

____

EDUCATION IN THE COLONIES

New England parents wanted their children to read the Bible. They made laws requiring the education of children and set up town schools.

The colonists also founded Harvard College to teach ministers.

CHALLENGE ACTIVITY

Critical Thinking: Develop Develop three questions about the Pilgrims' contributions and research to answer them.

Anne Hutchinson	Mayflower Compact	Puritans
immigrants	Pilgrims	Tisquantum
John Winthrop		

DIRECTIONS Answer each question by writing a sentence that contains at least one word from the word bank.

1. Who was put on trial for his or her religious ideas and eventually forced out of the colony?

____

____

2. Who are people that leave their country of birth to live in another country?

____

____

3. Who showed the Pilgrims how to fertilize the soil on their farms and helped them establish relations with the chief of the local Wampanoag Indians?

____

____

4. Who led a group of Puritan colonists who left England for Massachusetts in search of religious freedom?

____

____

5. What Protestant group wanted to reform, or purify, the Church of England?

____

____

DIRECTIONS Choose at least five of the terms or names from the word bank. Use these words to write a letter that relates to the lesson.

Lesson 3

MAIN IDEAS

1. The English created New York and New Jersey from former Dutch territory.
2. William Penn established the colony of Pennsylvania.
3. The economy of the middle colonies was supported by trade and staple crops.

Key Terms and People

Peter Stuyvesant director general who led the New Netherland colony beginning in 1647

Quakers (Society of Friends) a religious group that believed in the equality of men and women before God; supported nonviolence and religious tolerance

William Penn a Quaker leader who founded the Pennsylvania colony

staple crops crops that are always needed, such as wheat, barley, and oats

Lesson Summary

NEW YORK AND NEW JERSEY

In 1613 the Dutch formed New Netherland as a base for trading fur with the Iroquois. They traded fur mostly in the town of New Amsterdam on Manhattan Island. Large land grants and religious tolerance meant Jews, French Huguenots, Puritans, and others came to the colony.

What was the first town on Manhattan Island?

____

Why did the Dutch settle New Amsterdam?

____

____

Director-general **Peter Stuyvesant** ruled the colony beginning in 1647. In 1664 an English fleet gained control of New Netherland without any fighting. New Amsterdam became New York City, named in honor of the Duke of York. New York was the first of the middle colonies.

The Duke of York made two men proprietors, or governors, of New Jersey. The colony was located between the Hudson and Delaware rivers. Dutch, Finns, Swedes, Scots, and others lived there.

Underline the sentence that makes you think the population of New Jersey was diverse.

PENN'S COLONY

One of the largest religious groups in New Jersey was the Society of Friends, or the **Quakers**. Their religious practices were different from other groups since they did not follow formal religious practices. They believed in the equality of men and women before God. They also backed religious tolerance for all groups. The Quakers' beliefs angered many Christians. Quakers were treated badly in both England and America.

William Penn started a colony named Pennsylvania. He offered religious freedom to all Christians. He created a way to change colony laws based on what the people wanted. Many Quakers settled in Pennsylvania. Penn named his capital Philadelphia, which means "the city of Brotherly Love."

What does *Philadelphia* mean?

____

ECONOMY OF THE MIDDLE COLONIES

A good climate and fertile land meant the colonists could grow a large quantity of **staple crops**, unlike colonists in New England. Some slaves worked in the middle colonies but not as many as in the south. Indentured servants did more of the labor.

By the 1700s Philadelphia and New York City had grown into large cities. Trade was important to the middle colonies. Women ran some farms and businesses such as clothing and grocery stores. Other women also became nurses and midwives.

How did the middle and southern colonies differ?

____

____

____

CHALLENGE ACTIVITY

Critical Thinking: Evaluate Think about the middle colonies. How are they similar? How are they different? Decide which colony you would like to live in. Then write a short essay explaining why you chose the colony you did. Illustrate your essay.

Peter Stuyvesant	Quakers	staple crops	William Penn

DIRECTIONS Use all the vocabulary words from the word bank to write a summary of what you learned in this lesson.

____

____

____

____

____

____

____

____

____

____

DIRECTIONS Read each sentence and fill in the blank with the word in the word pair that best completes the sentence.

1. Director-general ____________________ controlled the colony of New Netherland beginning in 1647. (William Penn/Peter Stuyvesant)
2. ____________________ are items that are always needed, such as wheat and barley. (Staple crops/Cash crops)
3. The ____________________supported the equality of men and women before God, religious tolerance, and nonviolence. (Dutch/Quakers)
4. Pennsylvania was established by ____________________ to provide a government that was fair to all people. (William Penn/the Dutch)
5. The economy of the middle colonies depended on the production of ____________________, skilled labor, and trade. (tobacco/staple crops)

Name ______________________ Class ______________ Date __________

The English Colonies

Lesson 4

MAIN IDEAS

1. Colonial governments were influenced by political changes in England.
2. English trade laws limited free trade in the colonies.
3. The Great Awakening and the Enlightenment led to ideas of political equality among many colonists.
4. The French and Indian War gave England control of more land in North America.

Key Terms and People

town meeting assembly in which colonists decided issues and made laws

English Bill of Rights act passed in 1689 that reduced the powers of the English monarch and gave Parliament more power

triangular trade system in which goods and slaves were traded among the Americas, Britain, and Africa

Great Awakening religious movement in the colonies during the 1730s and 1740s

Jonathan Edwards important leader of the Great Awakening; from Massachusetts

Enlightenment movement during the 1700s that spread the idea that reason and logic could improve society

John Locke philosopher who thought that people had natural rights

Pontiac Native American leader who led a rebellion in the Ohio Valley in 1763

salutary neglect policy in which Britain interfered very little in colonial affairs

Lesson Summary

COLONIAL GOVERNMENTS

The House of Burgesses, Virginia's second assembly, helped make laws. Its members were elected by colonists. In New England, colonists at **town meetings** decided local issues. The middle colonies used both county and town meetings.

King James II of England thought the colonies were too independent. He united the northern colonies and limited their powers. In 1689 the **English Bill of Rights** shifted power from the monarch to Parliament, the British governing

How were laws made in Virginia and New England?

____

____

____

Did the colonists benefit from the English Bill of Rights? Why?

____

____

body. These rights were not extended to the colonists.

ENGLISH TRADE LAWS

England controlled its colonies to earn money. Parliament passed the Navigation Acts, that forced colonists to trade only with Britain. Some colonists wanted to trade at markets with the best prices.

One version of the **triangular trade** involved colonists trading rum for slaves from the African coast. The slave trade forced millions of Africans across the Atlantic Ocean in a voyage called the Middle Passage. Thousands of slaves died.

What is the name given to the voyage of slaves from Africa to America?

____

GREAT AWAKENING AND ENLIGHTENMENT

During the **Great Awakening**, talk of spiritual equality made some people, such as **Jonathan Edwards**, think about social and political equality. **Enlightenment** thinker **John Locke** said people should obey their rulers only if the state protected life, liberty, and property.

FRENCH AND INDIAN WAR

In 1675 a war erupted between colonists and the Wampanoag. Metacomet, or King Philip, was opposed to the colonists' taking Indian lands. The fighting ended after both colonists and Indians died.

Underline King Philip's real name.

The French and Indian War was about the British wanting to settle in the Ohio Valley and the French wanting it for the fur trade. After the war, Britain won Canada and all French lands east of the Mississippi River.

Native American leaders opposed British settlements in the Ohio Valley. Chief **Pontiac** led followers against the British. He later gave up, but King George III banned colonists from settling on Indian lands. Many settlers ignored

How did many Americans react to the king's ban on settling on Indian lands?

____

____

the ban because they were used to **salutary neglect**.

CHALLENGE ACTIVITY

Critical Thinking: Make Inferences Imagine you live during the Enlightenment. Write a short journal entry describing the time.

DIRECTIONS Look at each set of four terms. On the line provided, write the letter of the term that does not relate to the others.

______ 1. a. House of Burgesses
b. town meetings
c. Parliament
d. Great Awakening

______ 2. a. Navigation Acts
b. English Bill of Rights
c. trade
d. markets

______ 3. a. slavery
b. triangular trade
c. John Locke
d. Middle Passage

______ 4. a. spiritual equality
b. Jonathan Edwards
c. Great Awakening
d. salutary neglect

______ 5. a. triangular trade
b. Metacomet
c. French and Indian War
d. Pontiac

DIRECTIONS Write two adjectives or descriptive phrases that describe each term.

6. House of Burgesses ____

____

7. Jonathan Edwards ____

____

8. French and Indian War ____

____

9. English Bill of Rights ____

____

10. Great Awakening ____

Name ______________________ Class ______________ Date __________

The American Revolution

Lesson 1

MAIN IDEAS

1. British efforts to raise taxes on colonists sparked protest.
2. The Boston Massacre caused colonial resentment toward Great Britain.
3. Colonists protested the British tax on tea with the Boston Tea Party.
4. Great Britain responded to colonial actions by passing the Intolerable Acts.

Key Terms and People

Committees of Correspondence method of communication between towns and colonies about how to challenge new British laws

Samuel Adams Boston leader who believed Parliament could not tax the colonists without their permission

Stamp Act of 1765 required colonists to pay for an official stamp when buying paper items

Mercy Otis Warren writer in the Massachusetts colony who wrote plays that accused British leaders of being greedy

Boston Massacre shootings by British soldiers that killed five colonists

Tea Act an act allowing a British company to sell cheap tea directly to the colonists

Boston Tea Party a protest in which colonists dressed as Native Americans and dumped over 340 tea chests from British ships into Boston Harbor

Intolerable Acts laws passed to punish colonists for the Boston Tea Party

Quartering Act required colonists to house British soldiers

Lesson Summary

GREAT BRITAIN RAISES TAXES

Parliament raised the colonists' taxes for money to pay for the French and Indian War. The tax money was also used to help pay for a British army to protect the colonists against American Indian attacks. Parliament also tried harder to arrest smugglers avoiding taxes.

Name one reason that Parliament raised taxes.

____

____

____

Many colonists believed Britain had no right to tax them without their permission. Colonists communicated their ideas about British laws in **Committees of Correspondence**. **Samuel Adams** and James Otis inspired the slogan "No Taxation without Representation." Colonists refused to buy British goods. They hoped Parliament would end the new taxes. The **Stamp Act of 1765** meant a tax had to be paid on documents. In protest, **Mercy Otis Warren** wrote plays that accused the British leaders of being greedy.

How did colonists respond to British taxes?

____

____

The Townshend Acts charged taxes on imported glass, lead, paint, paper, and tea. Boston's Sons of Liberty attacked the houses of customs officials to protest the taking of a ship on suspicion of smuggling. British soldiers came to Boston in 1768 to restore order.

Underline the sentence that tells what the Townshend Acts did.

BOSTON MASSACRE

On March 5, 1770, a group of soldiers fired on Bostonians who were throwing snowballs at them. Colonists called it the **Boston Massacre**. The soldiers and their officer were charged with murder. A jury found the officer and six soldiers acted in self-defense and were not guilty. Two soldiers were convicted of accidental killing. This calmed Boston for a while.

Why do you think the jury found some of the troops not guilty?

____

____

____

THE BOSTON TEA PARTY

Parliament ended almost all of the Townshend Acts but left the tax on tea. Colonists united against the **Tea Act**. In November 1773 the **Boston Tea Party** showed the colonists' spirit of rebellion.

THE INTOLERABLE ACTS

The Boston Tea Party made the British prime minister very angry. Parliament punished Boston by passing the **Intolerable Acts**. The laws closed Boston Harbor until the colonists paid for the lost tea. A new **Quartering Act** required colonists to house British soldiers. Other parts of the Intolerable Acts angered the colonists even more.

Why did the Boston Tea Party anger the British prime minister?

____

____

CHALLENGE ACTIVITY

Critical Thinking: Summarize Imagine you write for Boston's Committees of Correspondence. Give a brief description of the Boston Massacre.

DIRECTIONS Match the definition in the first column with the letter of the correct term in the second column.

______ 1. These groups were created to share information with other towns and colonies about ways to challenge new British laws.

______ 2. In this event, colonists disguised as Native Americans dumped more than 340 tea chests into Boston Harbor.

______ 3. These laws were designed to punish the colonists in Boston for their actions against the British.

______ 4. This man wrote and circulated papers encouraging colonists to join the protest against unfair taxation.

______ 5. This took place when British soldiers fired into a crowd, killing five colonists.

______ 6. This woman wrote plays accusing the British of being greedy.

a. Boston Massacre
b. Boston Tea Party
c. Committees of Correspondence
d. Intolerable Acts
e. Mercy Otis Warren
f. Samuel Adams

DIRECTIONS Read each sentence. Choose which of the pair of answers given best completes the sentence and fill in the blank.

7. Samuel Adams helped found the ______________________, which shared ideas and information about the new British laws and ways to challenge them. (House of Burgesses/Committees of Correspondence)

8. The ______________________ required colonists to pay for an official stamp, or seal, whenever they bought paper items. (Townshend Acts/Stamp Act)

9. As part of the ____, Boston Harbor was closed until colonists paid for tea destroyed in the Boston Tea Party. (Intolerable Acts/Tea Act)
10. The ____________________________________ was used as propaganda against the British by Samuel Adams and other protestors. (Boston Massacre/Boston Tea Party)
11. ____________________________________ helped create the Sons of Liberty to protest and use violence to frighten tax collectors. (Samuel Adams/ James Otis)
12. A new ____ required colonists to house British soldiers. (Stamp Act/Quartering Act)

Name ______________________ Class ______________ Date __________

Lesson 2

MAIN IDEAS

1. The First Continental Congress demanded certain rights from Great Britain.
2. Armed conflict between British soldiers and colonists broke out with the "shot heard 'round the world."
3. The Second Continental Congress created the Continental army to fight the British.
4. In two early battles, the army lost control of Boston but then regained it.

Key Terms and People

First Continental Congress gathering of colonial leaders who were deeply troubled about the relationship between Great Britain and its colonies in America

Patriots colonists who chose to fight for independence

Redcoats British soldiers wearing red uniforms

minutemen members of the local militia who were ready to fight at a minute's notice

Second Continental Congress meeting of delegates from 12 colonies in Philadelphia in May 1775

Continental army army created by the Second Continental Congress to carry out the fight against Britain

George Washington the Virginian who commanded the Continental army

Battle of Bunker Hill battle won by the British but with double the losses of the Patriots

Lesson Summary

FIRST CONTINENTAL CONGRESS

Delegates to the **First Continental Congress** were worried about the relationship between Great Britain and the American colonies. The delegates debated whether violence was avoidable. They encouraged the peaceful boycott of British goods. However, they also began preparing for war. They drafted a Declaration of Rights to present to King George III. Colonists who chose to fight for independence were known as **Patriots**.

What did the delegates debate?

____

____

"SHOT HEARD 'ROUND THE WORLD"

In April 1775 the **Redcoats** set out for Concord. A British general sent the soldiers to destroy a stockpile of weapons they thought was there. Three colonists rode out on horseback to warn that the British were coming. Seventy armed **minutemen** waited for the British at Lexington. To this day, nobody knows who fired the first shot. The British killed eight minutemen, then went on to Concord where they destroyed a few buildings. In reaction, the minutemen fired on the Redcoats. The British suffered many casualties and were forced to retreat.

Why did the British soldiers go to Concord?

____

____

SECOND CONTINENTAL CONGRESS

At the **Second Continental Congress**, some delegates called for war while others wanted peace. The Congress named the Massachusetts militia the **Continental army**. The army's commander was **George Washington**. Delegates signed the Olive Branch Petition asking King George to make peace. He would not consider it.

What was King George's response to the Olive Branch Petition?

____

____

EARLY BATTLES

On June 17, 1775, the British in Boston found colonial forces dug in on Breed's Hill. When the British crossed the harbor in boats, the colonists opened fire. In the battle, now known as the **Battle of Bunker Hill**, the British won. But the Battle of Bunker Hill proved the colonists could fight. Soon after, General Washington took command of the Continental army in Boston. He set up cannons from Fort Ticonderoga to fire on the British. On March 7, 1776, the British retreated from Boston.

What was the battle fought near Breed's Hill called?

____

____

CHALLENGE ACTIVITY

Critical Thinking: Draw Conclusions Why do you think the first shot at Lexington was called the "shot heard 'round the world"?

DIRECTIONS Read each sentence and fill in the blank with the word in the word pair that best completes the sentence.

1. The ________________________________ chose not to break away from Britain but did create a military force and a new currency with which to pay the soldiers. (First Continental Congress/Second Continental Congress)
2. General George Washington led the main colonial military force, which was called the ________________________________. (Continental army/ minutemen)
3. Delegates to the ________________________________ drafted a Declaration of Rights to be presented to King George. (First Continental Congress/Second Continental Congress)
4. Members of the local militia of Massachusetts were known as ________________________________. (minutemen/Redcoats)
5. Although the colonists lost, the ________________________________ proved that they could take on the British. (Battle of Bunker Hill/Siege of Fort Ticonderoga)

DIRECTIONS Write two adjectives or descriptive phrases that describe the term, person, or event.

6. Battle of Bunker Hill ________________________________

____

7. George Washington ________________________________

____

8. minutemen ________________________________

____

9. Redcoats ________________________________

____

10. Second Continental Congress ________________________________

____

Name ______________________________ Class ____________________ Date _____________

Lesson 3

MAIN IDEAS

1. Thomas Paine's *Common Sense* led many colonists to support independence.
2. Colonists had to choose sides when independence was declared.
3. The Declaration of Independence did not address the rights of all colonists.

Key Terms and People

Common Sense a 47-page pamphlet that argued against British rule over America

Thomas Paine author of *Common Sense* who wrote that citizens, not monarchs, should make laws

Thomas Jefferson the main author of the Declaration of Independence

Declaration of Independence the document that formally announced the colonies' break from Great Britain

Loyalists colonists, sometimes called Tories, who remained loyal to Britain

Lesson Summary

PAINE'S *COMMON SENSE*

Common Sense was a pamphlet published anonymously. Written by **Thomas Paine**, it expressed his views that citizens, not kings, should pass laws. As word of the pamphlet spread throughout the colonies, it eventually sold about 500,000 copies. The pamphlet made a strong case for political and economic freedom. It supported the right to military self-defense. *Common Sense* changed the way many colonists viewed their king.

Why do you think *Common Sense* was so popular?

____

____

INDEPENDENCE IS DECLARED

The first point argued by **Thomas Jefferson** in the **Declaration of Independence** was that all men possess unalienable rights. Unalienable rights are rights that cannot be denied. These rights include "life, liberty, and the pursuit of happiness." Jefferson maintained that King George III had trampled on the colonists' rights with unfair laws and meddling in colonial governments. Jefferson argued that the colonies had the right to be independent from Britain. He believed in the Enlightenment idea of the social contract. This idea says that citizens should agree to be governed only when governments support their rights. Jefferson said that King George III had violated the social contract, so the colonies should not obey his laws.

Why did Jefferson think the colonies should not obey King George III?

____

____

____

On July 4, 1776, the Continental Congress voted in favor of the Declaration of Independence. In approving the Declaration, the Congress finally broke away from Great Britain. Today we celebrate the Fourth of July as the birthday of our nation.

What did some families experience during the war?

____

____

____

Not everyone rejoiced over the approval of the Declaration. Patriots and **Loyalists** became divided. Sometimes family members were on opposite sides during the war. More than 50,000 Loyalists left the colonies during the Revolution.

UNFINISHED BUSINESS

The Declaration did not mention certain colonists. Abigail Adams, wife of delegate John Adams, tried to influence him to include women's rights in the Declaration. It did not happen. Enslaved African Americans also had no rights under the Declaration. Slavery was legal in all colonies in July 1776. The Revolutionary War would not end the fight over slavery, even though New England states worked toward ending it in the 1780s.

Name two groups who had no rights under the Declaration.

____

____

CHALLENGE ACTIVITY

Critical Thinking: Develop Imagine that you are a delegate to the Second Continental Congress. Deliver a two-minute speech arguing that the Declaration should also give women and enslaved people rights.

Common Sense	Patriots	Thomas Paine
Declaration of Independence	Thomas Jefferson	unalienable
Loyalists		

DIRECTIONS Answer each question by writing a sentence that contains at least one term from the word bank.

1. What did Thomas Paine write to encourage the colonists to declare independence?

____

____

2. What did the Second Continental Congress do to formally declare the colonies free from Great Britain?

____

____

3. What group of colonists faced hostility because they sided with the British?

____

____

4. Who was the main author of the Declaration of Independence, and what three main points did he make in the document?

____

____

____

____

Lesson 4

MAIN IDEAS

1. Many Americans supported the war effort.
2. The Patriots both won and lost battles during the years 1775–1777.
3. France and Spain helped the Patriots fight the British.
4. The winter at Valley Forge tested the strength of Patriot troops.
5. The war continued at sea and in the West.

Key Terms and People

Haym Salomon immigrant from Poland who spied for the Patriots and later used his skills as a banker to help fund the American Revolution

mercenaries foreign soldiers who fought not out of loyalty, but for pay

Battle of Trenton a battle won by the Patriots against Hessian mercenaries

Battle of Saratoga a great victory for the American forces in which British general John Burgoyne surrendered his entire army to American general Horatio Gates

Marquis de Lafayette a Frenchman who volunteered to serve in the Continental army without pay and used his money and influence to support the Patriots

Baron Friedrich von Steuben a Prussian military officer who trained the Continental army

Bernardo de Gálvez the governor of Spanish Louisiana who became a Patriot ally

John Paul Jones naval commander who said, "I have not yet begun to fight!"

George Rogers Clark a surveyor who led the Patriots' western campaign

Lesson Summary

SUPPORTING THE WAR EFFORT

Life in the army was hard, but the Patriots knew they were fighting for an important cause. More than 230,000 men served in the Continental army. After the British promised to free any enslaved people who fought for them, the Continental army allowed free African Americans to serve. Women played an important role in the war by helping to supply the army and serving as messengers, nurses, and spies.

Underline the sentence that tells how some women served the war effort.

DEFEATS AND VICTORIES

At first, the Continental army lost several battles. Soldiers combined under the leadership of generals Richard Montgomery and Benedict Arnold were defeated in Canada. In New York City, General George Washington and his troops were forced to retreat. When the city was captured, **Haym Salomon**, an immigrant from Poland, stayed there and spied for the Patriots.

After those defeats, the Patriots won an important victory. British General Howe, who thought the rebellion would soon be over, left New Jersey in the hands of Hessian **mercenaries**. The Patriots surprised the Hessians and won the **Battle of Trenton**.

British general John Burgoyne planned to cut off New England from the other colonies. His strategy required perfect timing. The Patriots surrounded Burgoyne and won the **Battle of Saratoga**, which was the turning point of the war.

How did Haym Salomon help the cause of the Patriots?

____

____

Circle the names of two battles won by the Patriots.

HELP FROM EUROPE

Britain's enemies, France and Spain, began to help the Patriots. A wealthy Frenchman, the **Marquis de Lafayette**, brought well-trained soldiers on his own ship. He volunteered to serve in the Continental army without pay. **Baron Friedrich von Steuben**, an experienced military officer from Prussia, trained American troops. **Bernardo de Gálvez**, governor of Spanish Louisiana, became a key ally to the Patriots.

Why would France and Spain help the Patriots?

____

____

____

WINTER AT VALLEY FORGE

The winter of 1777 turned brutally cold and snowy. General Washington settled his troops at Valley Forge. They bore hardships with courage and drilled to become better soldiers.

WAR AT SEA AND IN THE WEST

The British lost hundreds of ships to the small Continental navy. **John Paul Jones** fought a battle with the British in which his ship took heavy damage. He fought on, and the British ship *Serapis* surrendered. In the West, **George Rogers Clark** led Patriots against British trading villages and Fort Sackville. Clark's campaigns hurt British support in the West.

What effect did Clark's campaigns have on the British?

____

____

CHALLENGE ACTIVITY

Critical Thinking: Elaborate Write and perform a dialogue between two soldiers discussing their hard times at Valley Forge.

Baron Friedrich von Steuben	Bernardo de Gálvez	John Paul Jones
Battle of Saratoga	George Rogers Clark	Marquis de Lafayette
Battle of Trenton	Haym Salomon	mercenaries

DIRECTIONS Read each sentence. Choose which of the pair of answers given best completes the sentence and fill in the blank.

1. In the ______________________________, the Patriots crossed the Delaware River in a successful surprise attack on Hessian mercenaries.
2. ______________________________ spied for the Patriots in New York, and later used his skills as a banker to help fund the American Revolution.
3. A French nobleman, the ______________________________, brought soldiers to America and volunteered to fight in the Continental army.
4. ______________________________ are foreign soldiers who are paid to fight.
5. The ______________________________ in eastern New York was an important turning point in the war.
6. The Continental navy Patriot sailor who gained fame when he captured the British warship *Serapis* was ______________________________.
7. ______________________________ was the governor of Spanish Louisiana who became a Patriot ally.

8. A Prussian military officer named ______________________________ trained soldiers in the Continental army.
9. In the West, ______________________________'s campaigns hurt British support.

Name ______________________________ Class __________________ Date __________

Lesson 5

MAIN IDEAS

1. Patriot forces faced many problems in the war in the South.
2. The American Patriots finally defeated the British at the Battle of Yorktown.
3. The British and the Americans officially ended the war by signing the Treaty of Paris of 1783.

Key Terms and People

Francis Marion a Patriot leader who used hit-and-run attacks, known as guerilla warfare

James Armistead an enslaved African who worked as a spy and provided information that gave the Continental army an advantage at Yorktown

Comte de Rochambeau commander of 4,000 French troops that aided the Patriot forces at the Battle of Yorktown

Battle of Yorktown the last major battle of the American Revolution

Treaty of Paris of 1783 the peace agreement in which Great Britain recognized the independence of the United States

Lesson Summary

WAR IN THE SOUTH

The war in the northern colonies did not go as the British government had hoped. The northern Patriots were tough to beat. The British moved the war into the South, where they believed large groups of Loyalists would help them win. General Henry Clinton led the British troops. The British plan worked at first.

Why did the British move the war to the South?

____

____

____

The war in the South proved especially brutal. Patriots and Loyalists engaged in direct fighting. The British wiped out crops, farm animals, and property. Georgia fell to the British. Next, the British conquered the port of Charleston, South Carolina. The Patriots failed to retake Camden, South Carolina.

Underline the sentence that explains how the British army waged war in the South.

Patriot general Nathanael Greene arrived to shape up the army. Meanwhile, under the leadership of **Francis Marion**, the Southern Patriots used surprise attacks to cut off British communication and supply lines. The British could not capture Marion and his men.

How did Francis Marion and his men hurt the British?

____

____

____

BATTLE OF YORKTOWN

The Patriots were in trouble in early 1781. They had little money for paying soldiers and buying supplies. The British held most of the South as well as Philadelphia and New York.

The Continental army began to pressure the British in the Carolinas. General Charles Cornwallis moved his 7,200 men to Yorktown, Virginia.

Why did Cornwallis move his troops to Yorktown?

____

____

An enslaved African named **James Armistead** was a spy for the Continental army. As a result of information he provided, General Washington saw a chance to trap Cornwallis at Yorktown. Washington combined his troops with French troops commanded by **Comte de Rochambeau** (raw-shahn-BOH). Washington led the French-American force to Virginia.

With 16,000 soldiers, Washington's force surrounded Cornwallis. For weeks, the French-American force wore down the British troops. Finally, the British surrendered. The Patriots captured 8,000 British prisoners at the **Battle of Yorktown**.

THE TREATY OF PARIS

Britain lost most of its army at Yorktown and could not afford a new one. So Great Britain and America began peace talks. Delegates took more than two years to reach a peace agreement.

Why might reaching a peace treaty have taken so long?

____

____

____

The **Treaty of Paris of 1783** gave the United States independence from Great Britain. It also created America's borders. In a separate treaty, Britain returned Florida to the Spanish. The Patriots' courage had won the Revolutionary War.

CHALLENGE ACTIVITY

Critical Thinking: Predict Imagine that the Patriots had lost the Revolutionary War. Help lead a class discussion on how your lives would be different today.

DIRECTIONS Read each sentence. Choose which of the pair of answers given best completes the sentence and fill in the blank.

1. The British moved the war into the South, where they believed large groups of ______________________________ would help them win. (Patriots/ Loyalists)
2. Under the leadership of ______________________________, the Southern Patriots used surprise attacks to cut off British communication and supply lines. (Francis Marion/James Armistead)
3. General ______________________________ led the British army at Yorktown. (Henry Clinton/George Cornwallis)
4. ______________________________ was a spy who provided information that gave the Continental army an advantage at Yorktown. (James Armistead/Comte de Rochambeau)
5. General George Washington combined his troops with French troops commanded by ______________________________. (George Cornwallis/Comte de Rochambeau)
6. The British surrendered at the Battle of ______________________________. (Charleston/Yorktown)
7. Peace talks between Great Britain and America took ______________________________ to reach an agreement. (two days/ two years)
8. The Treaty of Paris of 1783 gave the United States independence from ______________________________. (Great Britain/France)

Name ______________________ Class ______________ Date __________

Forming a Government

Lesson 1

MAIN IDEAS

1. The American people examined many ideas about government.
2. The Articles of Confederation laid the base for the first national government of the United States.
3. The Confederation Congress established the Northwest Territory.

Key Terms and People

Magna Carta an English document, signed by King John in 1215, that limited the power of the monarch

constitution a set of basic principles and laws that states the powers and duties of the government

suffrage voting rights

Virginia Statute for Religious Freedom a law that included Thomas Jefferson's ideas granting religious freedom

Articles of Confederation the new national constitution, which made a new Confederation Congress the national government

ratification official approval by the states

Land Ordinance of 1785 a law that set up a system for surveying land and dividing the Northwest Territory

Northwest Ordinance of 1787 a law that established the Northwest Territory and formed a political system for the region

Northwest Territory a territory including Illinois, Indiana, Michigan, Ohio, and Wisconsin

Lesson Summary

IDEAS ABOUT GOVERNMENT

After winning independence from Great Britain, the United States needed to form new governments. The Americans first looked to English law for ideas. The English Bill of Rights and the **Magna Carta** gave them inspiration. Ideas from the Enlightenment also influenced them. English philosopher John Locke wrote that the government had a duty to guard people's rights.

Where did Americans find ideas for their government?

____

____

____

In 1639 the people of Connecticut created a government plan considered to be the first written **constitution** in the colonies. During the American Revolution nearly every state wrote a constitution to ensure that citizens elected representatives to make laws. **Suffrage** varied considerably from state to state. Some constitutions banned slavery. The **Virginia Statute for Religious Freedom** was an example of a law providing religious freedom.

Which state produced a government plan considered to be the first written constitution in the colonies?

____

ARTICLES OF CONFEDERATION

The Continental Congress named a Committee of Thirteen, with one member from each colony. This committee drafted the **Articles of Confederation**.

Under the Articles the Confederation, Congress had limited powers to guard the people's freedoms. Each state had one vote in Congress. Congress had powers, but it could ask the states only for money and soldiers. States could refuse these requests. After some conflicts the Articles were sent to each state for **ratification**, or official approval. All the states approved, and formed the first American government.

Why would you have voted for or against the Articles?

____

____

____

NORTHWEST TERRITORY

Congress decided to raise money to pay debts by selling the western lands it controlled. Congress passed the **Land Ordinance of 1785**. The **Northwest Ordinance of 1787** formed the **Northwest Territory**. It was then split up into several smaller territories. When the population of a territory hit 60,000, its settlers could draft their own constitution and ask to join the Union. Slavery was banned in the Northwest Territory.

Underline the sentence that explains when a territory could ask to join the Union.

CHALLENGE ACTIVITY

Critical Thinking: Elaborate You plan to settle in the Northwest Territory. List ten items you will take with you and explain why you chose the items you did.

Articles of Confederation	Magna Carta
constitution	Virginia Statute for Religious Freedom

DIRECTIONS Read each sentence and choose the correct term from the word bank to replace the underlined phrase. Write the term in the space provided and then define the term in your own words.

1. The <u>Land Ordinance of 1785</u> was the national constitution created by the 13-member committee appointed by the Second Continental Congress.

   Your definition: ________________________________

   ____

2. The <u>English Bill of Rights</u>, which included Jefferson's ideas about religious freedom, stated that no Virginian would be forced to attend a particular church or to pay for one with tax money.

   Your definition: ________________________________

   ____

   ____

3. The <u>Northwest Territory</u>, which limited the power of England's kings and queens, was signed by King John in 1215.

   Your definition: ________________________________

   ____

4. A <u>Virginia Statute for Religious Freedom</u> is a set of basic principles and laws that states the powers and duties of the government.

   Your definition: ________________________________

   ____

Name ______________________ Class ______________ Date __________

Forming a Government

Lesson 2

MAIN IDEAS

1. The United States had difficulties with other nations.
2. Internal economic problems plagued the new nation.
3. Shays's Rebellion pointed out weaknesses in the Articles of Confederation.
4. Many Americans called for changes in the national government.

Key Terms and People

tariffs taxes on imports or exports

interstate commerce trade between two or more states

inflation increased prices combined with the reduced value of money

depression a period of low economic activity combined with a rise in unemployment

Daniel Shays a poor farmer and Revolutionary War veteran

Shays's Rebellion a 1786 uprising in which Daniel Shays led hundreds of men in a forced shutdown of the Supreme Court in Springfield, Massachusetts

Lesson Summary

RELATIONS WITH OTHER COUNTRIES

The Continental army broke up soon after the signing of the Treaty of Paris of 1783. The Articles of Confederation provided no way to raise a new army. The United States had a hard time guarding against foreign threats.

Problems arose in trading with Britain, which closed many British ports to U.S. ships. The British also forced American merchants to pay high **tariffs**. U.S. merchants increased prices to pay them, and costs were passed on to customers.

In 1784 Spanish officials shut down the lower Mississippi River to U.S. shipping. Western farmers and merchants used the river to ship goods east and overseas. The U.S. government failed to work out an agreement with Spain. Critics thought Spain would have negotiated longer if America had a strong military force. The loss of the British West Indies markets

Point out one weakness in the Articles of Confederation.

____

____

____

Why did tariffs hurt U.S. citizens?

____

____

____

meant farmers could not sell goods there. U.S. exports dropped, while lower-priced British goods kept entering America. Congress could not pass tariffs.

ECONOMIC PROBLEMS

Trade problems among the states, war debt, and a poor economy hurt the states. The Confederation Congress had no power to regulate **interstate commerce**. States looked out only for their own trade interests.

Underline the sentence that lists problems facing the states.

In addition, states had trouble paying off war debts. They printed paper money, but it had no gold or silver backing and little value. This caused **inflation**, which occurs when increased prices for goods and services combine with the reduced value of money. The loss of trade with Britain coupled with inflation created a **depression**.

What conditions caused a depression in the United States?

____

____

____

SHAYS'S REBELLION

Massachusetts collected taxes on land to pay its war debt. This policy hurt farmers who owned land. The courts made them sell their property to pay taxes. **Daniel Shays** led an uprising of farmers to protest high taxes and heavy debt. That action was called **Shays's Rebellion**. Fourteen of the men involved were sentenced to death. However, the state freed most, including Shays. Many citizens agreed with Shays.

How would having to sell their land affect farmers?

____

____

____

CALLS FOR CHANGE

Shays's Rebellion pointed out weaknesses in the Articles of Confederation. Leaders, including James Madison and Alexander Hamilton, asked all 13 states to send delegates to a Constitutional Convention. It was held in Philadelphia in May 1787 to revise the Articles of Confederation and create a better constitution.

CHALLENGE ACTIVITY

Critical Thinking: Predict Consider how the new U.S. Constitution might change the Articles of Confederation. List three key changes.

Daniel Shays	inflation	Shays's Rebellion
depression	interstate commerce	tariffs

DIRECTIONS Answer each question by writing a sentence that contains at least one word from the word bank.

1. What happens when there is an increase in prices for goods and services combined with a reduction in the value of money?

____

____

2. What do we call taxes on imports and exports?

____

____

3. What revolt was started by farmers who believed they shouldn't have to sell their land to pay their taxes?

____

____

4. What do we call a period of low economic activity combined with a rise in unemployment?

____

____

5. Who was the leader of the group of farmers that forced a shutdown of the Supreme Court in Springfield, Massachusetts, in 1786?

____

____

6. What do we call trade between two or more states?

____

____

Name ______________________________ Class ____________________ Date ____________

Forming a Government

Lesson 3

MAIN IDEAS

1. The Constitutional Convention met to improve the government of the United States.
2. The issue of representation led to the Great Compromise.
3. Regional debate over slavery led to the Three-Fifths Compromise.
4. The U.S. Constitution created federalism and a balance of power.

Key Terms and People

Constitutional Convention meeting held in Philadelphia to create a new constitution

James Madison delegate from Virginia known as the "Father of the Constitution"

Virginia Plan a plan giving supreme power to the central government and creating a bicameral legislature made of two groups, or houses, of representatives

New Jersey Plan a plan creating a unicameral, or one-house, legislature

Great Compromise an agreement that gave each state one vote in the upper house of the legislature and a number of representatives based on its population in the lower house

Three-Fifths Compromise only three-fifths of a state's slaves were counted when deciding representation in Congress

popular sovereignty the idea that political power belongs to the people

federalism the sharing of power between a central government and the states

legislative branch a Congress of two houses that proposes and passes laws

executive branch the president and the departments that help run the government

judicial branch a system of all the national courts

checks and balances a system that keeps any branch of government from becoming too powerful

Lesson Summary

CONSTITUTIONAL CONVENTION

The **Constitutional Convention** met in May 1787 in Philadelphia, where America had declared independence. Twelve states sent delegates. Most

Name one reason Philadelphia was chosen as the site of the Convention.

____

____

delegates were educated and had served in state legislatures or Congress. **James Madison** of Virginia had good ideas about government and was able to lead the delegates to agreement.

GREAT COMPROMISE

States disagreed about representation, tariffs, slavery, and strength of the central government. In the **Virginia Plan**, two groups of representatives would be selected on the basis of each state's population. The **New Jersey Plan** proposed a one-house legislature in which each state received the same number of votes. The **Great Compromise** gave every state, regardless of size, an equal vote in the upper house of the legislature. Each state would be represented in the lower house based on population.

In which plan would there be only one group, or house, of representatives?

____

____

THREE-FIFTHS COMPROMISE

The **Three-Fifths Compromise** satisfied northerners, who wanted the number of slaves in southern states to determine taxes but not representation. It also satisfied southern delegates, who wanted slaves counted as part of their state populations to increase their power. The delegates agreed to end the slave trade in 20 years.

Underline the sentence that explains what action the delegates took about the slave trade.

A NEW SYSTEM OF GOVERNMENT

The delegates wanted to protect **popular sovereignty**. They thought **federalism** could accomplish that. States would control government functions not assigned to the federal government.

The Constitution balances power among the **legislative branch**, the **executive branch**, and the **judicial branch**. The Constitution's framers established **checks and balances** to prevent any one branch from becoming too strong. The Constitution was completed in September 1787.

What is the purpose of checks and balances?

____

____

____

CHALLENGE ACTIVITY

Critical Thinking: Make Judgments Decide whether you support the Great Compromise. Give a two-minute speech about your view.

DIRECTIONS Match the terms in the first column with their correct definitions from the second column by placing the letter of the correct definition in the space provided before each term.

_____ 1. checks and balances

_____ 2. Constitutional Convention

_____ 3. Great Compromise

_____ 4. James Madison

_____ 5. New Jersey Plan

_____ 6. popular sovereignty

_____ 7. Three-Fifths Compromise

_____ 8. Virginia Plan

_____ 9. federalism

_____10. legislative branch

a. meeting where delegates discussed ways to improve the Articles of Confederation

b. the sharing of power between a central government and the states it is comprised of

c. Virginia delegate called the Father of the Constitution

d. called for a two-house legislature with representation based on population

e. responsible for proposing and passing laws

f. called for a one-house legislature in which each state had an equal number of votes

g. gave each state an equal vote in the upper house of the legislature, while granting to the lower house representation based on population

h. agreement that only part of the slave population of a state would be used when determining representation

i. the idea that political authority belongs to the people

j. system by which any one branch of government is prevented from becoming too powerful

Name ______________________ Class ______________ Date ___________

Lesson 4

MAIN IDEAS

1. Federalists and Antifederalists engaged in debate over the new Constitution.
2. The *Federalist Papers* played an important role in the fight for ratification of the Constitution.
3. Ten amendments were added to the Constitution to provide a Bill of Rights to protect citizens.

Key Terms and People

Antifederalists people who opposed the Constitution

George Mason delegate who opposed the Constitution

Federalists people who supported the Constitution

Federalist Papers essays supporting the Constitution

amendments official changes to a document

Bill of Rights Constitutional amendments that protect the rights of citizens

Lesson Summary

FEDERALISTS AND ANTIFEDERALISTS

Antifederalists believed the Constitutional Convention should not have created a new government. Delegate **George Mason** opposed the Constitution because it did not contain a section that guaranteed individual rights.

Why did George Mason oppose the Constitution?

____

____

____

Most **Federalists** thought the Constitution provided a good balance of power. Some Antifederalists thought that the Constitution weakened states' rights and gave too much power to the central government.

Both Federalists and Antifederalists debated whether the new Constitution should be approved. Both groups made speeches advocating their views.

FEDERALIST PAPERS

The ***Federalist Papers*** were a series of essays defending the Constitution. Alexander Hamilton, James Madison, and John Jay wrote them anonymously. The writers tried to persuade people that the Constitution would not overwhelm the states. Madison wrote that the diversity of the United States would prevent any single group from dominating the government.

The Constitution needed only nine states to pass it. However, to preserve national unity, each state would ratify it. Every state except Rhode Island held state conventions to allow citizens to discuss and vote on the Constitution. On December 7, 1787, Delaware became the first state to ratify it. The Constitution went into effect in June 1788 after New Hampshire became the ninth state to ratify it. Several states ratified the Constitution only after a bill protecting individual rights was promised.

Why did states hold constitutional conventions?

____

____

____

What kind of bill did several states demand?

____

____

BILL OF RIGHTS

Many Antifederalists did not believe that the Constitution would safeguard personal rights. In the first session of Congress, James Madison urged the legislators to develop a bill of rights. The rights would then become **amendments** to the Constitution. Article V of the Constitution spelled out this way of changing the document.

In September 1789 Congress proposed 12 amendments. By December 1791 the states had ratified the **Bill of Rights**, ten of the proposed 12 amendments written to protect citizens' rights.

Why do you think the Constitution has lasted more than 200 years?

____

____

____

CHALLENGE ACTIVITY

Critical Thinking: Compare and Contrast Write a short essay comparing and contrasting the views of Federalists and Antifederalists. Use specific examples.

DIRECTIONS Read each sentence and fill in the blank with the word in the word pair that best completes the sentence.

1. A group of essays that defended the Constitution was the ______________________. (Bill of Rights/*Federalist Papers*)
2. ______________________ was an Antifederalist who felt the Constitution needed a bill of rights. (George Mason/Alexander Hamilton)
3. The ______________________ became the first ten amendments to the Constitution. (Bill of Rights/*Federalist Papers*)
4. Supporters of the Constitution were known as ______________________. (Federalists/Antifederalists)
5. People who felt the Constitutional Convention should not create a new government were called ______________________. (Federalists/Antifederalists)
6. ______________________ defended the Constitution in the *Federalist Papers*. (George Mason/Alexander Hamilton)
7. Official changes to the Constitution are called ______________________. (Bill of Rights/amendments)

Name ______________________ Class ______________ Date __________

Citizenship and the Constitution

Lesson 1

MAIN IDEAS

1. Delegates met at the Constitutional Convention to improve the government.
2. The Great Compromise and the Three-Fifths Compromise resolved controversial issues.
3. The new government was based on popular sovereignty, balance of power, and federalism.
4. Federalists and Antifederalists debated the Constitution.
5. The Constitution was ratified.

Key Terms and People

Constitutional Convention meeting held in Philadelphia to create a new constitution

James Madison a delegate from Virginia who contributed many ideas that shaped the Constitution

Virginia Plan a plan giving supreme power to the central government and creating a bicameral legislature made up of two groups, or houses, of representatives

New Jersey Plan a plan creating a unicameral, or one-house, legislature

Great Compromise an agreement that gave each state one vote in the upper house of the legislature and a number of representatives based on its population in the lower house

Three-Fifths Compromise only three-fifths of a state's slaves were counted when deciding representation in Congress

popular sovereignty the idea that political power belongs to the people

legislative branch a Congress of two houses that proposes and passes laws

executive branch the president and the departments that help run the government

judicial branch a system of all the national courts

checks and balances a system that keeps any branch of government from becoming too powerful

federalism the sharing of power between a central government and the states

amendments official changes to a document

Federalists people who supported the Constitution

Federalist Papers essays supporting the Constitution

Antifederalists people who opposed the Constitution

Bill of Rights constitutional amendments that protect the rights of citizens

Lesson Summary

CONSTITUTIONAL CONVENTION

The **Constitutional Convention** met in May 1787 with the goal of improving the Articles of Confederation. Fifty-five delegates attended. Most delegates were educated and had served in state legislatures or Congress. **James Madison** from Virginia attended.

What was the goal of the Constitutional Convention?

____

____

____

GREAT COMPROMISE

As the Convention began, the delegates disagreed about what form the government would take. The **Virginia Plan** proposed a legislature made up of two houses of representatives. States with more people would have more representatives. States with fewer people would have fewer representatives. The **New Jersey Plan** called for a one-house legislature in which each state received the same number of votes. The **Great Compromise** gave every state, regardless of size, an equal vote in the upper house of the legislature. Each state would be represented in the lower house based on population.

How did the Great Compromise give states representation?

____

____

____

COMPROMISES ON SLAVERY

Because representation in the House of Representatives would be based on the population of each state, the delegates had to decide who would be counted. The southern states had many more slaves than the northern states. The **Three-Fifths Compromise** was an agreement that three-fifths of the slave population would be counted. This satisfied northerners, who wanted the number of slaves in southern states to determine taxes but not representation. It also satisfied southern delegates, who wanted slaves counted as part of their state populations to increase the number of delegates they could have.

Underline the sentences that tell how both northerners and southerners could accept the Three-Fifths Compromise.

A NEW SYSTEM OF GOVERNMENT

The delegates wanted to protect **popular sovereignty**. The government was divided into three branches: **legislative branch**, **executive branch**, and **judicial branch**. The three branches include a system of **checks and balances**. This keeps any branch of the government from becoming too powerful. To balance power between national and state governments, the delegates created the system of **federalism**. States would control government functions not assigned to the federal government. Because the government might need to change in the future, a plan was included for making **amendments** to the Constitution.

What power did federalism give to state governments?

____

____

____

FEDERALISTS AND ANTIFEDERALISTS

The people who supported the Constitution took the name **Federalists** because the Constitution was based on federalism. They promoted their views in a series of essays known as the ***Federalist Papers***. Other people, called **Antifederalists**, thought the Constitution took too much power away from the states.

RATIFYING THE CONSTITUTION

Antifederalists wanted written guarantees that the people would have their individual freedoms protected. In the end, Federalists agreed and promised to add a **Bill of Rights** if the states ratified the Constitution. The Constitution was officially ratified in June 1788.

What was promised if the Constitution was ratified?

____

____

____

CHALLENGE ACTIVITY

Critical Thinking: Make Inferences How are the principles of popular sovereignty and federalism evident in the government of the United States?

Bill of Rights	checks and balances	executive branch
federalism	*Federalist Papers*	Great Compromise
judicial branch	popular sovereignty	Three-Fifths Compromise
Virginia Plan		

DIRECTIONS Answer each question by writing a sentence that contains at least one word from the word bank.

1. In what part of the government are the president and the departments that help run the government?

____

____

2. What agreement satisfied both northerners and southerners when it came to counting the population of a state?

____

____

3. What term is used for the sharing of power between a central government and state governments?

____

____

4. How can citizens be sure that no one branch of government becomes too powerful?

____

____

5. How did people who supported the Constitution express their ideas?

____

____

6. What amendments to the Constitution protect individual freedoms?

____

____

Lesson 2

MAIN IDEAS

1. The framers of the Constitution devised the federal system.
2. The legislative branch makes the nation's laws.
3. The executive branch enforces the nation's laws.
4. The judicial branch determines whether or not laws are constitutional.

Key Terms and People

federal system the government system that gives certain powers to the federal government

impeach vote to bring charges of serious crimes against a president

veto cancel

executive orders commands from the president that have the power of law

pardons orders from the president that grant freedom from punishment

Thurgood Marshall the first African American Supreme Court justice, appointed in 1967

Sandra Day O'Connor the first female Supreme Court justice, appointed in 1981

Sonia Sotomayor the first Hispanic American Supreme Court justice, appointed in 2009

Lesson Summary

THE FEDERAL SYSTEM

Under the **federal system**, the U.S. Constitution divides powers between the states and the federal government. The Constitution gives the federal government delegated powers, including coining money. It gives state governments or citizens reserved powers, including forming local governments. Concurrent powers are shared by federal and state governments. These powers include taxing.

Congress has added powers under the elastic clause to handle new issues.

Describe concurrent powers.

____

____

LEGISLATIVE BRANCH

The federal government has three branches, each with distinct responsibilities. Congress, the legislative branch, has two parts. The House of Representatives has 435 members. A state's population determines the number of representatives for that state. Each state has two senators. They are elected statewide and represent the interests of the entire state.

What determines each state's number of representatives?

____

____

EXECUTIVE BRANCH

This branch enforces laws made by Congress. The president heads the branch. Americans elect a president every four years. Presidents are limited to two terms. The House of Representatives can **impeach** the president. The Senate tries the cases. Congress dismisses the president if he or she is found guilty.

The president and Congress work together. A president can **veto** a law passed by Congress. Congress can undo a veto with a two-thirds majority vote. The president issues **executive orders** to carry out laws affecting the Constitution and other areas. The president also issues **pardons**.

How can Congress undo a presidential veto?

____

____

JUDICIAL BRANCH

A system of federal courts with the U.S. Supreme Court at the head makes up this branch. Federal courts can undo a state or federal law if the court finds it unconstitutional. Congress can then change the law to make it constitutional.

If someone thinks a conviction was unfair, he or she can take the case to the court of appeals. The losing side in that trial may appeal the decision to the U.S. Supreme Court. If the Court declines to hear a case, the decision of the court of appeals is final. The Supreme Court has become more diverse with the appointments of

Why might a president appoint more diverse justices?

____

____

____

Thurgood Marshall, **Sandra Day O'Connor**, and **Sonia Sotomayor**.

CHALLENGE ACTIVITY

Critical Thinking: Make Judgments Would you prefer to serve in the House or the Senate during an impeachment? Write a brief essay explaining why.

DIRECTIONS On the line provided before each statement, write **T** if a statement is true and **F** if a statement is false. If the statement is false, rewrite it on the line provided so that it is a true statement.

_____ 1. The House of Representatives can impeach a president.

____

____

_____ 2. Congress can veto a law that the president passes.

____

____

_____ 3. The powers granted by the Constitution to the federal government are called delegated powers.

____

____

_____ 4. A vote to bring charges of "treason, bribery, or other high crimes and misdemeanors" against a president is called impeachment.

____

____

_____ 5. Sandra Day O'Connor became the first Hispanic American justice on the Supreme Court.

____

____

______ 6. The powers kept by the state governments or the citizens are called delegated powers.

____

____

______ 7. A president of the United States can be impeached.

____

____

______ 8. Thurgood Marshall became the first African American president of the United States.

____

____

Name ______________________________ Class ____________________ Date ____________

Citizenship and the Constitution

Lesson 3

MAIN IDEAS

1. The First Amendment guarantees basic freedoms to individuals.
2. Other amendments focus on protecting citizens from certain abuses.
3. The rights of the accused are an important part of the Bill of Rights.
4. The rights of states and citizens are protected by the Bill of Rights.

Key Terms and People

majority rule the idea that the greatest number of people in a society can make policies for everyone

petition a request made of the government

search warrant an order authorities must get before they search someone's property

due process a rule that the law must be fairly applied

indict formally accuse

double jeopardy a rule that says a person cannot be tried for the same crime more than once

eminent domain the power of the government to take personal property to benefit the public

Lesson Summary

FIRST AMENDMENT

James Madison began writing a list of amendments to the Constitution in 1789. The states ratified ten amendments called the Bill of Rights. **Majority rule** could take away smaller groups' rights.

What does the Bill of Rights do?

____

____

The Bill of Rights protects all citizens. First Amendment rights include freedom of religion. The U.S. government cannot support or interfere with the practice of a religion.

The First Amendment also includes freedom of the press. It says citizens have freedom of speech, of assembly, and the right to **petition**. The freedoms of speech and the press give Americans the right to express their own ideas and to hear those of others. Freedom of assembly means

Americans may hold lawful meetings. Citizens can petition for new laws.

PROTECTING CITIZENS

The Second Amendment gives state militias the right to bear arms in emergencies. The Third Amendment protects citizens against housing soldiers. The Fourth Amendment protects against "searches and seizures." Authorities must obtain a **search warrant** to enter a citizen's property.

When do authorities need a search warrant?

____

____

RIGHTS OF THE ACCUSED

The Fifth Amendment says that the government cannot punish anyone without **due process** of law. This means the law must be fairly applied. A grand jury decides whether there is enough evidence to **indict** a person. No one can face **double jeopardy**. Under **eminent domain** the government must pay owners a fair amount for their property.

The Sixth Amendment protects an indicted person's rights. The Seventh Amendment says that juries can decide civil cases about money or property. The Eighth Amendment allows bail, or money defendants pay if they fail to appear in court. This amendment also prevents "cruel and unusual punishments" against a person convicted of a crime.

Predict a situation in which a government might exercise its right of eminent domain.

____

____

____

RIGHTS OF STATES AND CITIZENS

The Ninth Amendment says that all citizens' rights are not given by the Constitution. The Tenth Amendment says the states and the people hold any powers not delegated to the federal government or prohibited to the states.

What powers are held by the states and the people?

____

____

____

CHALLENGE ACTIVITY

Critical Thinking: Develop In a small group, draw up a new law for which you would like to petition a government official.

DIRECTIONS Write two adjectives or descriptive phrases that describe each term.

1. double jeopardy ______________________________

____

2. due process ______________________________

____

3. eminent domain ______________________________

____

4. indict ______________________________

____

5. majority rule ______________________________

____

6. petition ______________________________

____

7. search warrant ______________________________

____

DIRECTIONS Write a word or phrase that means the opposite of the term given.

8. indict ______________________________
9. due process ______________________________
10. majority rule ______________________________

Name ______________________________ Class ____________________ Date __________

Lesson 4

MAIN IDEAS

1. Citizenship in the United States is determined in several ways.
2. Citizens are expected to fulfill a number of important duties.
3. Active citizen involvement in government and the community is encouraged.

Key Terms and People

naturalized citizens foreign-born people who: a) live in the United States, b) whose parents are not citizens, and c) who complete the requirements for U.S. citizenship

deport return to an immigrant's country of origin

draft required military service

political action committees groups that collect money for candidates who support certain issues

interest groups groups of people who share a common interest that motivates them to take political action

Lesson Summary

GAINING U.S. CITIZENSHIP

Foreign-born people whose parents are not citizens of the United States may become **naturalized citizens** of the United States. First, they apply for citizenship. Then they go through a process that leads to citizenship. When citizenship is granted, they have most of the rights and responsibilities of other citizens.

Legal immigrants have many of the rights and responsibilities of citizens. However, they cannot vote or hold public office. The U.S. government can **deport** immigrants who break the law. Legal immigrants over age 18 may seek naturalization after living in the United States for five years. After completing the requirements, the people stand before a naturalization court and take an oath of allegiance to the United States. They then receive certificates of naturalization. There are two differences between native-born and

What limits exist on the rights of legal immigrants?

____

____

Where is the oath of allegiance taken?

____

____

naturalized citizens. Naturalized citizens can lose their citizenships. Naturalized citizens cannot become president or vice-president.

RESPONSIBILITIES OF CITIZENSHIP

Citizens have duties as well as rights. Citizens must obey laws and authority. In addition, they must pay taxes for services. Taxes pay for public roads and public schools. Americans pay a tax on their income to the federal government. Sometimes they pay an income tax to their state. Men 18 years or older must register with selective service in case of a **draft**. Citizens must serve on juries to give others the right to a trial by jury.

Why do citizens have duties along with rights?

____

____

____

Voting in elections is one of a citizen's most important responsibilities. Before voting, a citizen must find out as much as possible about the issues and candidates. A variety of media sources offer information, but some may be deliberately biased.

Underline the sentence that describes the media.

CITIZENS AND SOCIETY

Anyone can help in a campaign, even people who are not eligible to vote. Many people help with donations to **political action committees** (PACs). People can influence government officials at any time, not just during elections. Many U.S. citizens work with **interest groups**. Citizens can also work alone in elections or politics in general.

Many dedicated Americans also volunteer in community service groups. Volunteer firefighters fight fires. Neighborhood Watch groups tell police if they see criminal activity. Simple acts such as picking up trash in a park or serving food at a food shelter help a community.

Why is community service important and valuable?

____

____

____

CHALLENGE ACTIVITY

Critical Thinking: Analyze What connects a citizen's rights and responsibilities? Design a graphic organizer showing connections.

DIRECTIONS Write two adjectives or descriptive phrases that describe each term.

1. interest groups ____

____

2. immigrants ____

____

3. political action committees _________________________________

____

4. naturalized citizens ____

____

5. draft ____

____

deport	draft	political action committees
immigrants	interest groups	naturalized citizens

DIRECTIONS Use the six vocabulary words above to write a summary of what you learned in the lesson.

____

____

____

____

____

____

____

____

____

____

Lesson 1

MAIN IDEAS

1. In 1789 George Washington became the first president of the United States.
2. Congress and the president organized the executive and judicial branches of government.
3. Americans had high expectations for their new nation.

Key Terms and People

George Washington an honest leader, a hero of the Revolution, and the first U.S. president

electoral college a group of delegates, or electors, who represent the people's vote in choosing the president

Martha Washington George Washington's wife and the First Lady

precedent an action or a decision that later serves as an example

Judiciary Act of 1789 an act that created three levels of federal courts and defined their powers and relationships to the state courts

Lesson Summary

THE FIRST PRESIDENT

George Washington was unanimously elected by the **electoral college** in January 1789. John Adams became his vice-president. **Martha Washington** entertained and accompanied her husband at social events. She was in charge of the presidential household. Other women, such as Abigail Adams, wife of John Adams, believed women needed to play a larger role in the new nation than Martha Washington did. They believed that mothers could teach their children to be good citizens.

Why did some women support a larger national role for women?

____

____

ORGANIZING THE GOVERNMENT

The new federal government had to establish a **precedent** when creating policies and procedures that would have a great influence on the future of the nation. Congress formed departments in the executive branch to oversee various areas of national policy. Washington consulted with

What did cabinet members provide for the president?

____

department heads, or cabinet members, who advised him. Our presidents today also meet with their key advisers.

Congress passed the **Judiciary Act of 1789**. This act created the federal court system and the courts' locations. The president nominates candidates for federal judgeships. The Senate holds the power to approve or reject the candidates.

What limited the president's ability to nominate federal judges?

____

____

AMERICANS' EXPECTATIONS FOR THE NATION

Americans had high expectations for their new country. They wanted trade that did not have the limits put in place by the British Parliament. They also expected the government to protect them and keep the economy strong.

In 1790 almost 4 million people lived in the United States. Most Americans worked on farms. They hoped for fair taxes and the right to move onto western lands. Americans who lived in towns worked as craftspeople, laborers, or merchants. They wanted help with their businesses. Merchants wanted simpler trade laws. Manufacturers wanted laws to shield them from overseas competitors.

Underline the sentences that explain the contrast between what country residents and town residents wanted.

What were the expectations of merchants and manufacturers?

____

____

Most cities were small. Only New York City and Philadelphia topped 25,000 residents. New York City, the first capital, reflected the new nation's spirit. In 1792 some 24 Wall Street stockbrokers signed an agreement that eventually created the New York Stock Exchange.

CHALLENGE ACTIVITY

Critical Thinking: Evaluate You have just attended George Washington's inauguration. Write a letter to a friend describing your thoughts about him.

electoral college	Judiciary Act of 1789	precedent
George Washington	Martha Washington	

DIRECTIONS Answer each question by writing a sentence that contains at least one term from the word bank.

1. What did Congress pass to set up the number of federal courts and their locations?

____

____

2. Who had to entertain guests and attend social events with the president of the United States?

____

____

3. What was the group of delegates called that was sent to choose the first president of the United States?

____

____

4. What do we call an action or a decision that later serves as an example?

____

____

Name ______________________ Class ________________ Date __________

Launching the Nation

Lesson 2

MAIN IDEAS

1. Hamilton tackled the problem of settling national and state debt.
2. Thomas Jefferson opposed Hamilton's views on government and the economy.
3. Hamilton created a national bank to strengthen the U.S. economy.

Key Terms and People

Alexander Hamilton the first secretary of the U.S. Treasury who wanted to pay the nation's foreign debt immediately and gradually repay the full value of all bonds

national debt money owed by the United States

bonds certificates that represent money

speculators people who buy items at low prices in the hope that the value will rise

Thomas Jefferson the first secretary of state who thought that repaying the full value of all bonds would cheat bondholders who had sold their bonds at low prices

loose construction the view that the federal government can take reasonable actions that the Constitution does not specifically forbid

strict construction the view that the federal government should do only what the Constitution specifically says it can do

Bank of the United States the national bank

Lesson Summary

SETTLING THE DEBT

Alexander Hamilton wanted to pay off the **national debt**. He figured that the United States owed $11.7 million to foreign countries. The nation also owed about $40.4 million to U.S. citizens.

During the Revolutionary War, the government sold **bonds** to raise money. Officials said bonds would be repurchased at a higher price. Some bondholders sold their bonds to **speculators**. Hamilton and **Thomas Jefferson** disagreed on what to do. More politicians agreed

How did the government raise money during the Revolution?

____

____

with Hamilton. The government replaced old bonds with new, more reliable ones.

Hamilton thought that the federal government should repay $21.5 million of the states' debt. But southern leaders objected. Their states had relatively low debts. Hamilton arranged to have the U.S. capital's location changed from New York to Philadelphia and finally Washington, DC. Southern leaders then supported his plan.

How did Hamilton persuade the southern leaders?

____

____

JEFFERSON OPPOSES HAMILTON

Hamilton and Jefferson disagreed about the role of the central government. Hamilton wanted a strong federal government. Jefferson wanted strong powers for the states. Hamilton did not want people to have much power because he had little faith in the average person. Jefferson believed that the people had the right to rule the country. Hamilton backed manufacturing, business, and higher tariffs. Jefferson backed farming and lower tariffs.

Underline the sentences that explain Hamilton's and Jefferson's views of the American people.

A NATIONAL BANK

In 1791 Hamilton and Jefferson disagreed about the government's economic problems. Hamilton wanted a national bank so the government could safely deposit money. Jefferson believed that Hamilton's plan gave too much power to the federal government. Hamilton supported **loose construction** of the Constitution. Jefferson backed **strict construction**. President Washington and Congress wanted the **Bank of the United States**. It helped make the U.S. economy more stable.

Name one reason Hamilton supported a national bank.

____

____

Do you think the national bank was a good idea? Why or why not?

____

____

____

CHALLENGE ACTIVITY

Critical Thinking: Evaluate Do you think Hamilton or Jefferson was more correct in his views of people? Give a brief speech explaining your opinion.

DIRECTIONS Read each sentence and fill in the blank with the word in the word pair that best completes the sentence.

1. ______________________ disagreed with the idea to pay speculators the full value of the government bonds that they had bought during the Revolutionary War. (Thomas Jefferson/Alexander Hamilton)
2. Hamilton's view of the Constitution was called ______________________. (loose construction/strict construction)
3. Congress chartered the ______________________, which played an important role in making the U.S. economy more stable. (national debt/Bank of the United States)
4. ______________________ are people who buy items at low prices in the hope that the value will rise. (Bonds/Speculators)
5. A ______________________ of the Constitution allows the federal government to take reasonable actions that the Constitution does not specifically forbid. (loose construction/strict construction)
6. People who favor ______________________ of the Constitution believe the federal government should do only what the Constitution says it can do. (loose construction/strict construction)
7. The amount of money that was owed by the United States was called the ______________________. (national debt/Bank of the United States)
8. The secretary of the treasury who had to deal with the challenge of paying off the national debt was ______________________. (Thomas Jefferson/Alexander Hamilton)
9. ______________________ are certificates that represent money. (Bonds/Speculators)
10. Thomas Jefferson's view of the Constitution was known as ______________________. (loose construction/strict construction)

Name ______________________ Class ______________ Date __________

Lesson 3

MAIN IDEAS

1. The United States tried to remain neutral regarding events in Europe.
2. The United States and Native Americans came into conflict in the Northwest Territory.
3. The Whiskey Rebellion tested Washington's administration.
4. In his Farewell Address, President Washington advised the nation.

Key Terms and People

French Revolution a rebellion of the French people against their king that led to the creation of a republican government

Neutrality Proclamation a formal statement that the United States would not take sides with any European countries who were at war

privateers private ships hired by a country to attack its enemies

Jay's Treaty an agreement that settled the disputes between the United States and Britain in the early 1790s

Pinckney's Treaty an agreement that settled border and trade disputes with Spain

Little Turtle a Native American chief who fought against U.S. forces in 1790

Battle of Fallen Timbers the battle that broke the strength of Native American forces in the Northwest Territory

Treaty of Greenville an agreement that gave the United States right of entry to American Indian lands

Whiskey Rebellion an uprising in which some farmers refused to pay the whiskey tax

Lesson Summary

REMAINING NEUTRAL

The **French Revolution** increased tensions between France and Britain. Many Americans supported the French Revolution, but others opposed it. France and Great Britain finally went to war. George Washington believed the United States should be neutral and issued the **Neutrality Proclamation**. A French representative asked American sailors to command **privateers** to aid

Why might some Americans support the French Revolution?

____

____

____

France in fighting England. Washington said that this violated U.S. neutrality. Jefferson thought the United States should support France and resented interference in his role as secretary of state. He resigned in 1793.

Washington wanted to stop a war between the United States and Britain. The two sides signed **Jay's Treaty**. Britain would pay damages on seized American ships. **Pinckney's Treaty**, signed with Spain, settled the issue of Florida's border and reopened New Orleans to American ships.

What did the United States gain from Pinckney's Treaty?

____

____

CONFLICT IN THE NORTHWEST TERRITORY

Americans continued to settle the territory despite protests of American Indians. U.S. forces lost a battle to Miami chief **Little Turtle**. But General Anthony Wayne commanded U.S. troops in gaining the territory at last. The American Indians were defeated in the **Battle of Fallen Timbers** and their leaders signed the **Treaty of Greenville** a year later.

Why might American Indians have protested the U.S. settlements?

____

____

____

THE WHISKEY REBELLION

In March 1791 Congress passed a tax on American-made whiskey. The **Whiskey Rebellion** broke out. Washington personally led the army against the rebels in western Pennsylvania, but they fled. The revolt ended with no battle.

WASHINGTON SAYS FAREWELL

Washington declined to run for a third term. He was tired of public life and considered the American people the nation's leaders. In his farewell speech, he warned about the dangers of foreign ties and political conflicts at home. He also cautioned against too much debt. At the conclusion of his speech, he stated that he looked forward to a life "of good laws under a free government . . ."

Name two dangers that Washington mentioned.

____

____

____

CHALLENGE ACTIVITY

Critical Thinking: Sequence Research events in this lesson to determine when each event occurred. Create a timeline. Describe each of the events and explain how one event caused or resulted from another event. Illustrate your timeline.

DIRECTIONS Match the terms in the first column with their correct definitions from the second column by placing the letter of the correct definition in the space provided before each term.

_____ 1. Battle of Fallen Timbers

_____ 2. French Revolution

_____ 3. Jay's Treaty

_____ 4. Little Turtle

_____ 5. Neutrality Proclamation

_____ 6. Pinckney's Treaty

_____ 7. privateers

_____ 8. Treaty of Greenville

_____ 9. Whiskey Rebellion

a. private ships hired by a country to attack its enemies

b. rebellion of the French people against their king

c. uprising in which some farmers refused to pay a tax on whiskey

d. where American Indians were defeated by the U.S. Army

e. ended the frontier war and gave the United States right of entry to American Indian lands in the Northwest Territory

f. said that Spain agreed to change the Florida border and that Spain's government would reopen the port at New Orleans to American ships

g. stated that the United States would not take sides with any European countries who were at war with one another

h. led an American Indian group that defeated U.S. forces in the Northwest Territory

i. signed by the United States and Great Britain; stated that the British would pay damages on seized American ships

Name ______________________ Class ________________ Date __________

Lesson 4

MAIN IDEAS

1. The rise of political parties created competition in the election of 1796.
2. The XYZ affair caused problems for President John Adams.
3. Controversy broke out over the Alien and Sedition Acts.

Key Terms and People

political parties groups that help elect people and shape politics

Federalist Party a political group that wanted a strong federal government and supported industry and trade

Democratic-Republican Party a political group that wanted to limit the federal government's powers

XYZ affair a French demand for a $250,000 bribe and a $12 million loan in exchange for a treaty

Alien and Sedition Acts laws meant to crush opposition war that deprived people of the freedom to say and write what they believed

Kentucky and Virginia Resolutions formal statements that argued that the Alien and Sedition Acts were unconstitutional

Lesson Summary

THE ELECTION OF 1796

In the election of 1796, more than one candidate ran for president. **Political parties** had started during Washington's presidency. Washington cautioned against party rivalry in his farewell, but rivalry dominated the 1796 election.

Alexander Hamilton was key in founding the **Federalist Party**. John Adams and Thomas Pinckney were the Federalist candidates. Thomas Jefferson and James Madison helped found the **Democratic-Republican Party**. That party selected Thomas Jefferson and Aaron Burr as its candidates.

Who helped start the Federalist Party?

____

Businesspeople in cities tended to support Adams. Farmers generally favored Jefferson. Both sides attacked each other. Adams won;

Jefferson was second. Adams and Jefferson then had to serve as president and vice-president.

PRESIDENT ADAMS AND THE XYZ AFFAIR

Adams made improving the relationship between the United States and France a high priority. France was unhappy when the United States refused to let its citizens join in the war against Britain. Adams sent U.S. diplomats to repair that problem and make a treaty to guard U.S. shipping. The French foreign minister refused to meet with them.

Three French agents said that the minister would discuss a treaty only if America paid a $250,000 bribe and gave a $12 million loan. The American public became furious about the **XYZ affair**, the name given to the demand for a bribe. Still, Adams did not declare war on France. This angered many other Federalists. At last the United States and France did negotiate a peace treaty.

Based on what you have read, what do you think Adams's view of France was?

____

____

____

In the end, what occurred between the United States and France?

____

____

THE ALIEN AND SEDITION ACTS

The **Alien and Sedition Acts**, passed by Federalists in Congress, became law in 1798. The Alien Act empowered the president to remove foreign residents he decided were involved in treason or secret plots against the government. The Sedition Act forbade U.S. residents to "write, print, utter, or publish" false or critical words against the government.

The **Kentucky and Virginia Resolutions** stated that the acts were unconstitutional. Jefferson and James Madison said that the states could disobey unconstitutional federal laws. Congress did not repeal the acts, though they were not renewed. The resolutions presented the view that states could dispute the federal government. Later, politicians would say this idea meant that the states could declare laws or actions of the federal government to be illegal.

Underline the sentence that explains what the Sedition Act did.

CHALLENGE ACTIVITY

Critical Thinking: Interpret Do some research on the Kentucky and Virginia Resolutions to discover when states maintained that they could declare federal law to be illegal. Write a brief essay explaining both sides of the argument.

DIRECTIONS Read each sentence and fill in the blank with the word in the word pair that best completes the sentence.

1. The president was allowed to remove foreign residents he thought were involved in treason or secret plots against the government by the ________________________. (Alien Act/Sedition Act)
2. The ____________________________________ said United States citizens could not "write, print, utter, or publish" false or hostile words against the government. (Alien Act/Sedition Act)
3. The bribe offer where French agents made unreasonable demands to U.S. diplomats is called the ____________________________________. (Federalist Party/XYZ affair)
4. Thomas Jefferson and James Madison helped start the ________________ ___________________, whose members were called Republicans. (Federalist Party/Democratic-Republican Party)
5. Alexander Hamilton helped found the ______________________________, which wanted a strong federal government. (Federalist Party/Democratic-Republican Party)

DIRECTIONS On the line provided before each statement, write **T** if a statement is true or **F** if a statement is false. If the statement is false, find a word or phrase in the lesson that makes the statement true. Write the new sentence on the line provided.

_____ 6. Groups that help elect people and shape policies are called the Alien and Sedition Acts.

____

____

_____ 7. The Federalist Party helped Alexander Hamilton, the man who helped found the party, get elected president of the United States in 1796.

____

____

_____ 8. In 1796 the Republicans chose Thomas Jefferson and Aaron Burr as their candidates.

____

____

Lesson 5

MAIN IDEAS

1. The election of 1800 marked the first peaceful transition in power from one political party to another.
2. President Jefferson's beliefs about the federal government were reflected in his policies.
3. *Marbury* v. *Madison* increased the power of the judicial branch of government.

Key Terms and People

John Adams Federalist president first elected in 1796 who lost the 1800 presidential election

Louisiana Purchase the purchase of Louisiana from France for $15 million, which roughly doubled the size of the United States

Meriwether Lewis a former army captain chosen by Jefferson to lead an expedition to explore the lands of the Louisiana Purchase

William Clark co-leader of the western expedition

Sacagawea Shoshone who helped the expedition by naming plants and gathering edible fruits and vegetables for the group

John Marshall a Federalist appointed by Adams to be Chief Justice of the Supreme Court

Marbury* v. *Madison a case that established the Supreme Court's power of judicial review

judicial review the Supreme Court's power to declare an act of Congress unconstitutional

Lesson Summary

THE ELECTION OF 1800

Thomas Jefferson defeated **John Adams** and became president in 1800. In campaigning, both sides had made their cases in newspaper editorials and letters. Both sides believed that if the other gained power, the nation would be destroyed.

How did the presidential candidates wage the campaign of 1800?

____

____

The campaigning was intense. Federalists said if Jefferson gained power, revolution and chaos would follow. Republicans claimed that Adams would crown himself king. Jefferson and Aaron Burr, his running mate, each won 73 votes. After the thirty-sixth ballot in the House of Representatives, the tie was broken and Jefferson was elected president.

JEFFERSON IN OFFICE

Jefferson gave his first speech in the new capital. He said he supported the will of the majority. He emphasized his belief in a limited government and the protection of civil liberties. Jefferson convinced Congress to let the Alien and Sedition Acts expire. He cut military spending to free money to pay the national debt. The Republican-led Congress passed laws to end the unpopular whiskey tax and other domestic taxes.

Name one action Jefferson took based on his principles.

____

____

____

In 1801 the national government was made up of only several hundred people. Jefferson liked it that way. He thought that safeguarding the nation against foreign threats, delivering the mail, and collecting custom duties were the most important functions of the federal government.

According to Jefferson, what were the most important functions of the federal government?

____

____

____

THE LOUISIANA PURCHASE

Jefferson wanted to expand the borders of the United States. One problem was that France controlled the Louisiana Territory, a huge area to the west of the Mississippi that included New Orleans. The port of New Orleans was essential for trade in an expanding country.

The French offered to sell the Louisiana Territory to the United States for just $15 million. That was a remarkable bargain, so the president and Congress agreed to the **Louisiana Purchase**.

What was the purpose of the Lewis and Clark expedition?

____

____

President Jefferson wanted Americans to learn more about the lands of the Louisiana Purchase. He asked **Meriwether Lewis** to lead an expedition to gather information about the territory. Lewis asked **William Clark** to join him.

Lewis and Clark and their crew traveled up the Missouri River. **Sacagawea** (sak-uh-juh-WEE-uh) and her husband aided Lewis and Clark, and eventually they reached the Pacific Ocean.

THE SUPREME COURT

Adams filled 16 new federal judgeships with Federalists before leaving office. Republicans in Congress soon repealed the Judiciary Act upon which Adams's appointments were based. A controversy arose because Adams appointed William Marbury as a justice of the peace. The documents supporting Marbury's appointment were not delivered while Adams was still in office.

When Jefferson took office, Secretary of State James Madison would not deliver them. Marbury sued and asked the Supreme Court to order Madison to give him the documents. **John Marshall** wrote the court's opinion in ***Marbury* v. *Madison***. He ruled that the law Marbury's case depended upon was unconstitutional. The case established the court's power of **judicial review**.

Why did Marbury sue Madison?

____

____

CHALLENGE ACTIVITY

Critical Thinking: Make Inferences What if the 1800 campaign were waged as campaigns are waged now? Write a speech that you think Thomas Jefferson would give. Deliver his speech.

DIRECTIONS Read each statement and choose the best answer from among the choices given. Circle the letter next to the answer you choose.

1. The two candidates for president in 1800 whose intense campaigns were waged in newspaper editorials and letters were
   a. John Marshall and Aaron Burr.
   b. Thomas Jefferson and John Adams.
   c. William Marbury and James Madison.

2. The Supreme Court's power to declare an act of Congress unconstitutional is
   a. federal judgeship.
   b. judiciary act.
   c. judicial review.
3. Thomas Jefferson considered all of the following important functions of government EXCEPT
   a. delivering the mail.
   b. charging a tax on whiskey.
   c. protecting the nation against foreign threats.
   d. collecting custom duties.
4. The men assigned to explore the new territory west of the Mississippi were
   a. Meriwether Lewis and William Clark.
   b. William Clark and William Marbury.
   c. John Adams and Thomas Jefferson.
5. The United States bought the Louisiana Territory from
   a. Great Britain.
   b. France.
   c. Spain.
6. Assisting the explorers who traveled through the new territory to the West was a Native American woman named
   a. Shoshone.
   b. Sacagawea.
   c. Louisiana.
7. The Supreme Court justice who wrote the court's opinion establishing the power of judicial review was
   a. John Marshall.
   b. William Marbury.
   c. James Madison.
8. The case that established the Supreme Court's power of judicial review was
   a. *Adams* v. *Jefferson.*
   b. *Lewis* v. *Clark.*
   c. *Marbury* v. *Madison.*

Name ______________________ Class ______________ Date __________

War and Expansion in the Americas

Lesson 1

MAIN IDEAS

1. Violations of U.S. neutrality led Congress to enact a ban on trade.
2. Native Americans, Great Britain, and the United States came into conflict in the West.
3. The War Hawks led a growing call for war with Great Britain.

Key Terms and People

USS *Constitution* a large U.S. warship sent to end attacks by the Barbary pirates on American merchant ships

impressment the practice of forcing people to serve in the army or navy

embargo the banning of trade

Embargo Act a U.S. law that essentially banned trade with all foreign countries

Non-Intercourse Act a new law banning only trade with Great Britain, France, and their colonies

Tecumseh a brilliant speaker who warned other Native Americans that settlers wanted their lands

Battle of Tippecanoe the battle between the U.S. forces and Tecumseh's followers that ended with the U.S. forces winning

War Hawks several members of Congress, led by Henry Clay, who called for war against Great Britain

James Madison a Republican who was elected president in 1808

Lesson Summary

VIOLATIONS OF NEUTRALITY

In the late 1700s and early 1800s, American merchant ships sailed the oceans. The profitable overseas trade was dangerous. Pirates from the Barbary States of North Africa seized cargo and held crews for ransom. The United States sent the **USS *Constitution*** and other ships to end the attacks.

When Great Britain and France declared war in 1803, each tried to stop the United States from selling goods to the other. The British and French searched many American ships for war goods. Then Britain started searching American ships

Why did Britain and France each try to stop the United States from selling goods to the other?

____

____

for sailors who had deserted the British navy. At times U.S. citizens were seized by accident.

Impressment continued over U.S. protests. Thomas Jefferson, who had been reelected in 1804, favored an **embargo** rather than war with Britain. In late 1807 Congress passed the **Embargo Act** to punish Britain and France. American merchants lost huge amounts of money because of the act, which prevented merchants from selling goods to either nation. In 1809 Congress replaced the embargo with the **Non-Intercourse Act**. That law did not work either.

How was an embargo an alternative to war?

____

____

____

CONFLICT IN THE WEST

In the West, Native Americans, the United States, and Great Britain clashed. As settlers poured into the West, Native Americans lost land that they believed was taken unfairly. British agents from Canada armed Native Americans in the West. **Tecumseh** (tuh-KUHM-suh), a Shawnee chief, united his forces with the Creek nation. William Henry Harrison, the governor of the Indiana Territory, raised an army to battle Tecumseh. At the daylong **Battle of Tippecanoe**, Harrison's forces defeated Tecumseh and his followers. Tecumseh fled to Canada.

How did British agents aid Native Americans in the West?

____

____

CALL FOR WAR

War Hawks in Congress led in demanding war against Britain. The leaders wanted to end British influence on Native Americans. They resented British restraints on U.S. trade. Others opposed war against Britain. They believed America lacked the military strength to win.

In 1808 Republican **James Madison** was elected president. He had difficulty carrying on the unpopular trade policy. In 1812 he asked Congress to vote on whether to wage war against Britain. Congress voted to declare war. Madison

Describe the problems that Madison faced in 1808.

____

____

____

was reelected and led the nation during the War of 1812.

CHALLENGE ACTIVITY

Critical Thinking: Predict What difficulties might the United States face in the War of 1812? List them.

DIRECTIONS Match the terms in the first column with their correct definitions from the second column by placing the letter of the correct definition in the space provided before each term.

______ 1. Battle of Tippecanoe

______ 2. embargo

______ 3. Embargo Act

______ 4. impressment

______ 5. Non-Intercourse Act

______ 6. Tecumseh

______ 7. USS *Constitution*

______ 8. War Hawks

______ 9. James Madison

a. sent by the United States to bring an end to the attacks by the Barbary pirates

b. the act of forcing people to serve in the army or navy

c. the banning of trade with a country

d. act that banned trade by the United States with all foreign countries

e. act that banned trade with Britain, France, and their colonies

f. a Shawnee chief

g. the all-day battle that resulted in Tecumseh fleeing to Canada

h. group of congressmen, led by Henry Clay, who called for war against Britain

i. Commander in Chief of the United States during the War of 1812

Lesson 2

MAIN IDEAS

1. American forces held their own against the British in the early battles of the war.
2. U.S. forces stopped British offensives in the East and South.
3. The effects of the war included prosperity and national pride.

Key Terms and People

Oliver Hazard Perry U.S. Navy commodore who won a victory against the British

Battle of Lake Erie the victory won by Perry and his sailors

Andrew Jackson the commander of the Tennessee militia who led an attack on the Creek nation in Alabama

Treaty of Fort Jackson the treaty that forced the Creek nation to give up millions of acres of their land

Battle of New Orleans the last major conflict of the War of 1812, which made Andrew Jackson a hero

Hartford Convention a meeting of Federalists opposed to the war

Treaty of Ghent the pact that ended the War of 1812

Lesson Summary

EARLY BATTLES

In 1812 the United States launched a war against Britain. The British navy had hundreds of ships. The U.S. Navy had fewer than 20 ships, but it boasted expert sailors and big new warships. American morale rose when its ships defeated the British in several battles. Finally, the British blockaded U.S. seaports.

Underline the sentences that contrast the U.S. and British navies.

The U.S. planned to attack Canada over land. The attack from Detroit failed when British soldiers and American Indians led by Tecumseh took Fort Detroit. Attacks from Niagara Falls and near Montreal failed when state militia troops refused to cross the Canadian border. They said they were not required to fight in a foreign country.

In 1813 the United States planned to end Britain's rule of Lake Erie. Commodore **Oliver Hazard Perry** and his small fleet won the **Battle of Lake Erie**. General Harrison then marched his troops into Canada. He defeated a combined force of British troops and Native Americans. Tecumseh died in the fighting, harming the alliance of the British and the Native Americans.

In 1814 **Andrew Jackson** won a battle against the Creek nation that ended in the **Treaty of Fort Jackson**.

What effect did the death of Tecumseh have?

____

____

____

GREAT BRITAIN ON THE OFFENSIVE

The British sent more troops to America after defeating the French in 1814. The British set fire to the White House and other buildings in Washington, DC. The British also attacked New Orleans.

Andrew Jackson commanded forces made up of regular soldiers. They included two battalions of free African Americans, a group of Choctaw Indian militia, and pirates led by Jean Lafitte. Although Jackson's forces were outnumbered, America won the **Battle of New Orleans**, the last key battle of the war. Andrew Jackson became a war hero.

Why was Andrew Jackson considered a hero?

____

____

____

EFFECTS OF THE WAR

A group of New England Federalists met in Connecticut. Known as the **Hartford Convention**, the Federalists agreed to oppose the war and sent delegates to Congress. Before the delegates reached Washington, the war had ended. Slow communications meant that neither Jackson nor the Federalists heard that the **Treaty of Ghent** finished the war. Each nation gave back the territory it had conquered. Two consequences of the War of 1812 were intense patriotism in America and growth of American manufacturing.

In what ways did the war benefit the United States?

____

____

____

CHALLENGE ACTIVITY

Critical Thinking: Make Inferences You are the first mate on a New England trading ship several months after the War of 1812. Write a letter about how the end of the war affects you.

DIRECTIONS Read each sentence. Choose which of the pair of answers given best completes the sentence, and fill in the blank.

1. The gathering in Connecticut of New England Federalists to oppose war is referred to as the ____________________________. (Treaty of Ghent/Hartford Convention)
2. The ____________________________ forced the Creek Indians to give up millions of acres of their land. (Battle of New Orleans/Treaty of Fort Jackson)
3. ____________________________ was the commander of the Tennessee militia that defeated the Creek Indians in Alabama. (Andrew Jackson/Oliver Hazard Perry)
4. ____________________________ led a small fleet that won the Battle of Lake Erie in 1813, which ended Britain's rule of Lake Erie. (Andrew Jackson/ Oliver Hazard Perry)
5. Although Jackson's forces were outnumbered, America won the ____________________________, the last key battle of the war. (Battle of Lake Erie/Battle of New Orleans)
6. Slow communications meant that neither Andrew Jackson nor the Federalists heard that the ____________________________ ended the war. (Treaty of Fort Jackson/Treaty of Ghent)

Lesson 3

MAIN IDEAS

1. The United States and Great Britain settled their disputes over boundaries and control of waterways.
2. The United States gained Florida in an agreement with Spain.

Key Terms and People

Rush-Bagot Agreement a compromise in 1817 that limited U.S. and British naval power on the Great Lakes

Convention of 1818 a treaty that gave the United States fishing rights off parts of the Newfoundland and Labrador coasts

James Monroe U.S. president elected in 1816

Adams-Onís Treaty an agreement that settled all border disputes between the United States and Spain

Lesson Summary

SETTLING DISPUTES WITH GREAT BRITAIN

After the War of 1812 ended, both the United States and Great Britain wanted to keep their navies on the Great Lakes. Both nations also wanted the rights to fish there.

The **Rush-Bagot Agreement** resolved that issue by limiting naval power on the Great Lakes. Both nations agreed to a limit of one or two ships on each lake.

Another treaty, the **Convention of 1818**, gave America certain fishing rights. It established the border between the United States and Canada. In this treaty both countries agreed to occupy the Pacific Northwest together.

What were the results of the Convention of 1818?

____

____

____

UNITED STATES GAINS FLORIDA

The United States also debated its border with Spanish Florida. Seminole Indians in Florida often aided runaway slaves. Sometimes they raided U.S. settlements. Encounters between Americans and Seminoles were unfriendly.

President **James Monroe** sent General Andrew Jackson and troops to protect the U.S.-Florida border. Under Jackson's command, U.S. troops invaded Florida to catch Seminole raiders. This started the First Seminole War. Without a direct command from the president, Jackson seized Spain's key military posts. The Spanish were upset, but most Americans backed Jackson.

Why did President Monroe send Jackson to Florida?

____

____

Jackson's presence in Florida convinced Spain to negotiate with the United States over ownership of Florida. In 1819 Secretary of State John Quincy Adams and Spanish diplomat Luis de Onís negotiated the **Adams-Onís Treaty**. This treaty settled all border disputes between the United States and Spain.

What convinced the Spanish to negotiate with the Americans?

____

____

____

CHALLENGE ACTIVITY

Critical Thinking: Identify Cause and Effect Make a chart identifying the causes and effects of the Rush-Bagot Agreement and Convention of 1818, and the Adams-Onís Treaty.

Adams-Onís Treaty	James Monroe
Convention of 1818	Rush-Bagot Agreement

DIRECTIONS Write two adjectives or descriptive phrases that describe the term.

1. Convention of 1818 ______________________________

____

____

2. James Monroe ______________________________

____

3. Rush-Bagot Agreement ______________________________

____

4. Adams-Onís Treaty ______________________________

____

DIRECTIONS Use the four vocabulary words to write a summary of what you learned in the section.

Name ______________________ Class ______________ Date __________

A New National Identity

Lesson 1

MAIN IDEAS

1. Success in foreign affairs contributed to a growing sense of American nationalism.
2. The Monroe Doctrine was a major shift in American Foreign Policy.

Key Terms and People

nationalism a sense of pride and devotion to a nation

Era of Good Feelings a U.S. era of peace, pride, and progress

Simon Bolívar the leader of the successful revolutions of Latin American colonies against Spain

Monroe Doctrine a statement of American policy warning European nations not to interfere with the Americas

Lesson Summary

GROWING NATIONALISM

Nationalism is a feeling of pride and loyalty to a nation. It is the belief that the interests of the whole nation are more important than regional interests or the interests of other countries.

James Monroe's presidency lasted for two terms, from 1817 to 1825. The economy of the United States grew rapidly. There was a spirit of nationalism among the people. One Boston newspaper called the time the "**Era of Good Feelings**."

How would a growing economy generate good feelings?

____

____

____

The good feelings at home were boosted by successes in foreign affairs. Americans were proud of their victory in the War of 1812. Problems with Britain and Spain over U.S. borders were solved. People felt settled and secure at home, and they would soon see a change in their country's foreign policy.

MONROE DOCTRINE

By the early 1820s most Latin American colonies had won independence from Spain. **Simon**

Bolívar, called the Liberator, led many of these battles. The U.S. saw the circumstances as similar to the American Revolution. United States leaders supported the Latin Americans in their struggles with European powers.

In 1921 Mexico won independence from Spain. Afterwards, President Monroe became afraid that European countries might try to take control of newly independent Latin American countries. He was also concerned that Russia was interested in the northwest coast of North America.

As a result he developed the **Monroe Doctrine**. This was new foreign policy for the United States. The Monroe Doctrine was a bold statement. It spelled out the relationship between European nations and the United States. The doctrine said that the United States would intervene in Latin American affairs when American security was at risk. Few European nations challenged the doctrine.

Why did the United States support Latin American independence?

____

____

____

What concerns did President Monroe have about other countries?

____

____

____

CHALLENGE ACTIVITY

Critical Thinking: Draw Conclusions Why do you think secure national borders were important to President Monroe?

Era of Good Feelings	nationalism
Monroe Doctrine	Simon Bolívar

DIRECTIONS Answer the following questions using terms from the word bank.

1. What name did a Boston newspaper use for the time of the Monroe presidency, and why?

____

____

____

2. How might someone describe the feelings of people who are very pleased with the country they live in? What might cause the people to feel that way?

____

____

____

3. Who was called "the Liberator," and what did he do?

____

____

____

4. How did President Monroe act on his concerns for the security of the United States and the Americas?

____

____

____

Name ______________________________ Class ____________________ Date ____________

A New National Identity

Lesson 2

MAIN IDEAS

1. Growing nationalism led to improvements in the nation's transportation systems.
2. The Missouri Compromise settled an important regional conflict.
3. The outcome of the election of 1824 led to controversy.

Key Terms and People

Henry Clay a U.S. representative from Kentucky who supported an emphasis on national unity

American System a series of measures intended to make the United States economically self-sufficient

Cumberland Road the first road built by the federal government

Erie Canal a waterway that ran from Albany to Buffalo, New York

sectionalism loyalty to the interests of one region of a country over the interests of the country as a whole

Missouri Compromise an agreement that settled the conflict over Missouri's application for statehood

John Quincy Adams chosen as president by the House of Representatives in 1824

Lesson Summary

NATIONALISM GUIDES DOMESTIC POLICY

Henry Clay supported nationalism. Clay developed the **American System** to create a stronger economy. He pushed for a national bank that would back a single currency to encourage interstate trade. He wanted a protective tariff to raise funds to improve roads and canals.

How might a single currency encourage interstate trade?

____

____

____

The dirt roads in the United States made travel hard. The **Cumberland Road** stretched from Maryland to the Ohio River in present-day West Virginia. By 1850 its extension reached Illinois.

Construction of the **Erie Canal** started in 1817 and was finished in 1825. Water transportation was often faster, less expensive, and easier than road travel. British, German, and Irish

Why were improvements in water transportation so important?

____

____

____

immigrants dug the entire canal using shovels and pickaxes. The Erie Canal allowed people and goods to travel between the Great Lakes region and New York City. The canal's success was an incentive for canal building across the country.

MISSOURI COMPROMISE

Disagreements between the North and South, known as **sectionalism**, threatened the Union. When Missouri applied to enter the Union, there were 11 free states and 11 slave states. The Senate's balance would favor the South if Missouri entered as a slave state.

Henry Clay persuaded Congress to agree to the **Missouri Compromise**. Missouri entered the Union as a slave state, and Maine entered as a free state. This kept an equal balance in the Senate. Slavery was banned in new territories or states north of Missouri's southern border.

How did Henry Clay help Missouri enter the Union?

____

____

____

THE ELECTION OF 1824

Senator Andrew Jackson gained the most popular votes but not enough electoral votes to win the election. The House of Representatives chose **John Quincy Adams** as president. Jackson's supporters claimed that Adams had made a "corrupt bargain" with Representative Henry Clay to win. Later, Adams named Clay secretary of state. The election controversy cost Adams support among Americans.

How did Andrew Jackson lose the election of 1824?

____

____

CHALLENGE ACTIVITY

Critical Thinking: Draw Conclusions Would you support Adams despite the Clay controversy? Why or why not?

DIRECTIONS Match the terms in the first column with their correct definitions from the second column by placing the letter of the correct definition in the space provided before each term.

_____ 1. American System

_____ 2. Cumberland Road

_____ 3. Erie Canal

_____ 4. sectionalism

_____ 5. Henry Clay

_____ 6. John Quincy Adams

_____ 7. Missouri Compromise

a. Henry Clay's plan to improve the U.S. economy

b. U.S. representative who was a strong supporter of national unity

c. allowed goods and people to move between the Great Lakes region and New York City

d. settled the conflict surrounding Missouri entering the Union

e. became president in 1824

f. disagreements between different regions

g. first road built by the federal government

A New National Identity

Lesson 3

MAIN IDEAS

1. American writers created a new style of literature.
2. A new style of art showcased the beauty of America and its people.
3. American ideals influenced other aspects of culture, including religion and music.
4. Architecture and education were affected by cultural ideals.

Key Terms and People

Washington Irving one of the first American writers to gain international fame

James Fenimore Cooper perhaps the best known of the new American writers

Hudson River school a group of artists whose paintings reflected national pride and an appreciation of the American landscape

Thomas Cole a landscape painter who was a founder of the Hudson River school

George Caleb Bingham an artist whose paintings showed both the American landscape and scenes from people's daily lives

Lesson Summary

AMERICAN WRITERS

Americans expressed their thoughts and feelings in literature and art. They took spiritual comfort in religion and music. The strengthening national identity was shown in education and architecture.

Washington Irving often wrote about American history. He cautioned Americans to learn from the past and prepare for the future. He often used a humorous style of writing called satire. In "Rip Van Winkle," one of his most famous short stories, Irving expresses his idea that Americans must use past lessons to deal with the future.

What was Irving's message?

____

____

____

James Fenimore Cooper wrote novels about characters who lived on the frontier, including Native Americans. His novels include *The Last of the Mohicans* and *The Pioneers*. By placing some characters in historical events, he popularized historical fiction.

A NEW STYLE OF ART

The works of Irving and Cooper inspired painters. By the 1830s the **Hudson River school** had appeared. The artists of the Hudson River school created beautiful paintings of the American landscape. **Thomas Cole** was a founder of the school. Other painters followed his lead. **George Caleb Bingham** and Alfred Jacob Miller traveled west to paint scenes of the American frontier, including trappers, traders, settlers, and Native Americans.

What subjects did American artists paint?

____

____

____

RELIGION AND MUSIC

Religious revivalism fanned out across America through the early and mid-1800s. Leaders met with large crowds to reawaken religious faith. People sang songs known as spirituals at revival meetings. Spirituals are a kind of folk hymn from both white and African American music traditions. Popular folk music showed the unique views of the nation. "Hunters of Kentucky" honored the Battle of New Orleans. It was used successfully in the presidential campaign of Andrew Jackson in 1828.

How were spirituals important for religious revival meetings?

____

____

____

ARCHITECTURE AND EDUCATION

In pre-Revolution America, most American architects modeled their designs on the style used in Great Britain. After the Revolution, Thomas Jefferson said that Americans should base their building designs on those of ancient Greece and Rome. Many architects agreed with Jefferson and used Greek and Roman styles.

Americans also found education important. In 1837 Massachusetts set up a state board of education. Other states followed Massachusetts and started their own education systems.

Why did Jefferson want Americans to change their styles of architecture?

____

____

____

CHALLENGE ACTIVITY

Critical Thinking: Elaborate Would you prefer to be a writer or a landscape artist? Make a choice, and either write an essay describing the western American landscape in the 1800s or draw a picture of it.

DIRECTIONS On the line provided before each statement, write **T** if a statement is true and **F** if a statement is false. If the statement is false, write the correct term on the line after each sentence that makes the sentence a true statement.

______ 1. One of the first American writers to gain international fame was Thomas Cole.

____

______ 2. James Fenimore Cooper wrote about characters who lived on the frontier and helped popularize historical fiction.

____

______ 3. A group of artists called the Hudson River school got its name because many of the artists' paintings showed the Hudson River valley.

____

______ 4. Washington Irving and Alfred Jacob Miller traveled west to paint scenes of the American frontier.

____

______ 5. James Fenimore Cooper was the leader of the Hudson River school.

____

______ 6. James Fenimore Cooper published novels such as *The Last of the Mohicans* and *The Pioneers*.

____

______ 7. Washington Irving used a humorous form of writing called satire to warn Americans that they should learn from the past and be cautious about the future.

____

The Age of Jackson

Lesson 1

MAIN IDEAS

1. Democracy expanded in the 1820s as more Americans held the right to vote.
2. Jackson's victory in the election of 1828 marked a change in American politics.

Key Terms and People

nominating conventions public meetings to select a party's presidential and vice presidential candidates

Jacksonian Democracy the democratic expansion that occurred because of Andrew Jackson's influence

Democratic Party a party formed by Jackson supporters

John C. Calhoun Jackson's vice presidential running mate

spoils system the practice of rewarding political supporters with government jobs

Martin Van Buren the secretary of state in Jackson's cabinet

Kitchen Cabinet an informal group of Jackson's trusted advisers that sometimes met in the White House kitchen

Lesson Summary

EXPANSION OF DEMOCRACY

Although Andrew Jackson was a popular political leader, he did not win the presidential election of 1824. Some people were disappointed because they believed he would defend the rights of the common people and slave states.

Why were some people disappointed when Andrew Jackson was not elected president?

____

____

____

Even though Andrew Jackson wasn't president, his supporters led Congress. During the time of Jackson's popularity, many democatic reforms were made. Some political parties began to hold **nominating conventions**, in which party members instead of party leaders chose candidates. This period of expanding democracy in the 1820s and 1830s became known as **Jacksonian Democracy**.

ELECTION OF 1828

Jackson supporters established the **Democratic Party**. Many supporters of President John Quincy Adams began calling themselves National Republicans.

The presidential candidates were President Adams and Jackson in a replay of the 1824 election. Jackson selected South Carolina senator **John C. Calhoun** as his running mate. The campaign concentrated on personalities. Jackson's campaigners said he was a war hero. He was born poor and earned success through hard work. They said that Adams knew nothing about everyday people. His father had been the second U.S. president. Adams's backers said Jackson was too coarse to be president.

Jackson and Calhoun won the election. Jackson's supporters described his victory as a triumph for the common people. After he was sworn in as president, a massive crowd followed Jackson to the White House lawn. They had a big party to celebrate. Jackson rewarded some of his supporters with government jobs. This was called the **spoils system**, but he replaced fewer than one-fifth of federal officeholders. One of Jackson's strongest allies in his cabinet was **Martin Van Buren**. Jackson relied on an informal group of trusted advisers called his **Kitchen Cabinet**.

Who established the Democratic Party?

____

What were some of the key differences between Jackson and Adams?

____

____

____

Why might so many people have attended the election party?

____

____

CHALLENGE ACTIVITY

Critical Thinking: Make Judgments Would you have supported Andrew Jackson or John Quincy Adams for president? Why or why not?

DIRECTIONS Read each sentence and fill in the blank with the word in the word pair that best completes the sentence.

1. Meetings to select the party's presidential and vice presidential candidates are called ____________________________. (Kitchen Cabinets/nominating conventions)
2. Secretary of State ____________________________ was one of President Andrew Jackson's strongest allies in his official cabinet. (John C. Calhoun/ Martin Van Buren)
3. The South Carolina senator that Andrew Jackson chose to be his vice presidential running mate was ____________________________. (John C. Calhoun/Martin Van Buren)
4. One group of trusted advisers to President Jackson, called the ____________________________, was an informal group that sometimes met in the White House. (Kitchen Cabinet/nominating convention)
5. A practice known as the ____________________________ was when an elected official rewarded some of his supporters with government jobs. (spoils system/nominating convention)

DIRECTIONS On the line provided before each statement, write **T** if a statement is true and **F** if a statement is false. If the statement is false, write the correct term on the line after each sentence that makes the sentence a true statement.

______ 6. The backers of <u>Andrew Jackson</u> were mostly farmers, frontier settlers, and southern slaveholders.

____

______ 7. The political party that supported Andrew Jackson was known as the <u>Democratic Party</u>.

____

______ 8. <u>John C. Calhoun</u> was elected president of the United States in 1828.

____

Name ______________________ Class ______________ Date__________

Lesson 2

MAIN IDEAS

1. Regional differences grew during Jackson's presidency.
2. The rights of the states were debated amid arguments about a national tariff.
3. Jackson's attack on the Bank sparked controversy.
4. Jackson's policies led to the Panic of 1837.

Key Terms and People

Tariff of Abominations the nickname given to a tariff by the southerners who opposed it

states' rights doctrine the belief that state power should be greater than federal power

nullification crisis the dispute over whether states had the right to nullify, or disobey, any federal law with which they disagreed

Daniel Webster a senator from Massachusetts who spoke out against nullification and believed the nation had to stay united

McCulloch* v. *Maryland the case in which the U.S. Supreme Court ruled that the Second Bank of the United States was constitutional

Whig Party a political group supported by people who opposed Andrew Jackson

Panic of 1837 a financial crisis that led to a severe economic depression

William Henry Harrison a general and the Whig presidential candidate in 1840

Lesson Summary

SECTIONAL DIFFERENCES INCREASE

In Andrew Jackson's presidency, people's reaction to almost every policy was based on where they lived. The North's economy depended on trade and manufacturing. The North supported tariffs, which helped it compete with foreign manufacturers. Southerners marketed a large portion of their crops to foreign countries. Most southerners opposed tariffs, which led to higher prices on items they bought. Westerners wanted cheap land.

Why did northerners disagree with southerners on the issue of tariffs?

____

____

____

Northerners continued to demand high tariffs to guard their new industries from foreign competition. Congress passed a law that southerners called the **Tariff of Abominations**. (An abomination is a hateful thing.) The tariff made sectional differences worse.

How did the Tariff of Abominations help industries in the North?

____

____

____

STATES' RIGHTS DEBATE

Early in his career, Vice President John C. Calhoun supported the idea of a strong central government. Later on, he argued for the **states' rights doctrine**. Calhoun believed that states had the right to nullify, or reject, any federal law they thought was unconstitutional. The debate over nullification led to the **nullification crisis**. **Daniel Webster** opposed nullification and backed a unified nation. Although opposed to nullification, Jackson was concerned about economic problems in the southern states. Henry Clay proposed a compromise that would lower the tariff gradually. Despite the compromise, neither side changed its beliefs about states' rights.

How did Jackson and Calhoun differ on the debate over states' rights?

____

____

____

JACKSON ATTACKS THE BANK

President Jackson and many southern states questioned the legality of the Second Bank of the United States. However, in the case ***McCulloch* v. *Maryland***, the Bank was found to be constitutional. Jackson moved most of the Bank's funds to state banks. This action caused inflation.

What happened when the federal bank's funds were moved to state banks?

____

____

PANIC OF 1837

The **Whig Party** backed four candidates for president in 1836. The Democrat, Martin Van Buren, won. When the country experienced the **Panic of 1837**, Van Buren was blamed. In 1840 the Whigs nominated **William Henry Harrison**, who won with an electoral landslide.

Why might voters have chosen Harrison over Van Buren?

____

____

____

CHALLENGE ACTIVITY

Critical Thinking: Summarize Design a poster that illustrates President Jackson's actions in his two terms. Use captions.

Daniel Webster	Panic of 1837	Whig Party
McCulloch v. *Maryland*	states' rights doctrine	William Henry Harrison
nullification crisis	Tariff of Abominations	

DIRECTIONS Answer each question by writing a sentence that contains at least one word from the word bank.

1. Which Supreme Court case upheld the constitutionality of the Second Bank of the United States?

____

____

2. What political party did William Henry Harrison belong to?

____

____

3. What rights did John C. Calhoun argue that tariffs violated?

____

____

4. What act, passed by Congress in 1828, resulted in increased sectional differences and the nullification crisis?

____

____

Name ______________________ Class ______________ Date__________

Lesson 3

MAIN IDEAS

1. The Indian Removal Act authorized the relocation of Native Americans to the West.
2. Cherokee resistance to removal led to disagreement between Jackson and the Supreme Court.
3. Other Native Americans resisted removal with force.

Key Terms and People

Indian Removal Act the act that authorized the removal of Native Americans who lived east of the Mississippi River

Indian Territory the new homeland for Native Americans, which contained most of present-day Oklahoma

Bureau of Indian Affairs an agency created to oversee the federal policy toward Native Americans

Sequoya a Cherokee who used 86 characters to represent Cherokee syllables to create a written language

Worcester* v. *Georgia a case in which the U.S. Supreme Court ruled that the state of Georgia had no authority over the Cherokee

Trail of Tears an 800-mile forced march westward in which one-fourth of the 18,000 Cherokee died

Black Hawk a leader of the Fox and Sauk who led his people in a struggle to protect their lands in Illinois

Osceola Seminole leader who called on Native Americans to resist removal by force

Lesson Summary

INDIAN REMOVAL ACT

President Andrew Jackson's policies toward Native Americans were controversial. Native Americans had long lived in settlements from Georgia to Mississippi. Jackson and other political leaders wanted this land for American farmers. Jackson pressured Congress to pass the **Indian Removal Act** in 1830. The **Indian Territory** was set aside as a new home for Native Americans. A new government agency, the

Why were Jackson's policies toward Native Americans controversial?

____

____

____

Bureau of Indian Affairs, was established to manage Indian removal to western lands.

The Choctaw were the first Indians sent to Indian Territory. Federal officials moved the Choctaw during a disastrous winter trip. There was not enough food or supplies. About one-fourth of the Choctaw died of cold, disease, or starvation.

What was the purpose of the Bureau of Indian Affairs?

____

____

____

News of the Choctaw's hardships caused other Indians to resist removal. However, the Cherokee believed they could prevent conflicts and avoid removal by adopting the culture of white people. Cherokee children learned to read and write English. **Sequoya** helped the Cherokee create their own written language.

How did the Cherokee believe they could avoid relocation?

____

____

After gold was discovered on Cherokee land, Georgia leaders began preparing to remove the Cherokee. Instead of responding with force, the Cherokee fought in court. They sued the federal government. In the case ***Worcester* v. *Georgia***, the U.S. Supreme Court ruled in favor of the Cherokee. Georgia ignored the ruling and removed the Cherokee. On the **Trail of Tears**, the Cherokee suffered from disease, hunger, and harsh weather.

How did the Cherokee fight the government?

____

____

____

OTHER NATIVE AMERICANS RESIST

Conflicts broke out in Illinois and Florida when some Native Americans decided to resist removal. **Black Hawk** led the Fox and Sauk of Illinois in a struggle to protect their lands. By 1850 they had been driven from the Illinois region.

In Florida the Seminole also resisted removal. Seminole leaders were forced to sign a treaty. Their followers decided to ignore it. A leader named **Osceola** led his followers in the Second Seminole War. The Seminole won many battles. U.S. officials decided to give up. Small groups of

How did the outcome for the Seminole differ from that of other Native Americans?

____

____

____

Seminole resisted removal, and their descendants still live in Florida today.

CHALLENGE ACTIVITY

Critical Thinking: Analyze Write an essay explaining how your view of the Indian Removal Act would compare or contrast with the view of an easterner who wanted to settle on Native American lands.

DIRECTIONS Write two adjectives or descriptive phrases that describe the term.

1. Black Hawk ____

____

2. Bureau of Indian Affairs ____

____

3. Indian Removal Act ____

____

4. Indian Territory ____

____

5. Osceola ____

6. Sequoya ____

____

7. *Worcester* v. *Georgia* ____

____

8. Trail of Tears ____

____

DIRECTIONS Read each sentence and fill in the blank with the word in the word pair that best completes the sentence.

9. Congress approved the creation of the ______________________ to oversee the federal policy toward Native Americans. (Bureau of Indian Affairs/ Indian Removal Act)

10. The Cherokee's 800-mile forced march from Georgia to Indian Territory became known as the ______________________. (Sequoya/Trail of Tears)

11. When U.S. officials ordered the removal of all American Indians from Illinois, Chief ______________________ decided to resist rather than leave. (Black Hawk/Sequoya)

Name ______________________ Class ________________ Date ___________

Westward Expansion

Lesson 1

MAIN IDEAS

1. As American settlers moved west, control of the Mississippi River became more important to the United States.
2. Expeditions led by Lewis, Clark, and Frémont increased Americans' understanding of the West.
3. During the early 1800s, Americans moved west of the Rocky Mountains to settle and trade.
4. Families moved into the far west and established thriving communities.

Key Terms and People

Daniel Boone guide who was first to lead settlers beyond the Appalachians; cut a road west

Louisiana Purchase the purchase of Louisiana from France for $15 million, which roughly doubled the size of the United States

Meriwether Lewis a former army captain chosen by President Thomas Jefferson to lead an expedition to explore the West

William Clark co-leader of the western expedition

Lewis and Clark expedition a long journey to explore the Louisiana Purchase

Sacagawea a Shoshone who helped the Lewis and Clark expedition by naming plants and gathering edible fruits and vegetables for the group

Zebulon Pike an explorer of the West who reached the summit of the mountain now known as Pike's Peak

John C. Frémont led an expedition to the Rocky Mountains in 1842 and wrote a report of his journey that became a guide for future travelers to the West

mountain men fur traders and trappers who traveled to the Rocky Mountains and the Pacific Northwest in the early 1800s

John Jacob Astor owner of the American Fur Company who founded the first important settlement in Oregon Country in 1811

Oregon Trail the main route from the Mississippi River to the West Coast in the early 1800s

Santa Fe Trail the route from Independence, Missouri, to Santa Fe, New Mexico

Mormons members of a religious group, formally known as the Church of Jesus Christ of Latter-day Saints, who moved west during the 1830s and 1840s

Brigham Young Mormon leader who chose Utah as the group's new home

Lesson Summary

THE FIRST WESTERNERS

In 1775 **Daniel Boone** led a group that cut a road west through the Cumberland Gap in Kentucky. Thousands of Americans moved to the area between the Appalachians and the Mississippi River. The setters used the Mississippi and Ohio rivers to move products east. New Orleans was an essential port for river trade. Spain governed New Orleans.

Why was the Mississippi River important?

____

____

LOUISIANA AND WESTERN EXPLORERS

In 1802 Spain shut American shipping out of New Orleans. Then they traded Louisiana to France. President Thomas Jefferson sent ambassadors to France. When the ambassadors tried to buy New Orleans, France offered to sell the entire territory of Louisiana. The United States bought the western territory for $15 million in the **Louisiana Purchase**.

Why did Jefferson send ambassadors to France?

____

____

President Jefferson wanted to learn more about the West and the Native Americans who lived there. He also wondered if there was a river route to the Pacific Ocean.

Underline the sentences that explain what Jefferson wanted to learn about the West.

In 1803 Congress provided money to explore the West. **Meriwether Lewis** and **William Clark** were chosen to lead the **Lewis and Clark expedition**, which began in May 1804.

Lewis and Clark and their crew traveled up the Missouri River. They saw Native Americans, and Lewis used interpreters to tell their leaders that the United States now owned the land on which they lived. **Sacagawea** (sak-uh-guh-WEE-uh) and her husband aided Lewis and Clark. Lewis and Clark did not find a river route to the Pacific, but they learned much about western lands.

What message did Lewis and Clark give to Native Americans?

____

____

____

In 1806 **Zebulon Pike** was sent to locate the Red River. The Red River was the Louisiana Territory's border with New Spain. In present-day Colorado he reached the summit of Pike's

Peak. Pike gave many Americans their first information about the Southwest.

Another explorer, **John C. Frémont**, led an expedition to the Rocky Mountains in 1842. He wrote a report of his journey that became a guide for future travelers. The information he gave made many more settlers eager to move west.

What was the result of John C. Frémont's report on his journey west?

____

____

____

MOUNTAIN MEN GO WEST

In the early 1800s trappers and traders known as **mountain men** worked to supply the eastern fashion for fur hats and clothing. **John Jacob Astor**, owner of the American Fur Company, sent mountain men to the Pacific Northwest region that became known as Oregon Country.

TRAILS WEST

Many Americans began to move to Oregon Country. Most of them followed a route that became known as the **Oregon Trail**. It was common for families to band together and undertake the perilous six-month journey in wagon trains.

Circle the names of three trails people used traveling west.

Mainly traders used another well-traveled route west, the **Santa Fe Trail**. They loaded wagon trains with cloth and other manufactured goods. They traded the goods for horses, mules, and silver in the Mexican settlement of Santa Fe.

One large group of settlers traveled to the West in search of religious freedom. They were known as **Mormons**, members of the Church of Jesus Christ of Latter-day Saints. Thousands of Mormons took the Mormon Trail. They traveled to an area near the Great Salt Lake in what is now Utah. **Brigham Young**, their leader, chose that site. By 1860 there were about 40,000 Mormons living in Utah.

What group traveled west in search of religious freedom?

____

CHALLENGE ACTIVITY

Critical Thinking: Draw Inferences Some members of the Lewis and Clark expedition kept journals or diaries. Write a brief diary entry as if you were a member of the expedition.

DIRECTIONS Match the terms in the first list with their correct definitions from the second list by placing the letter of the correct definition in the space provided before each term.

_____ 1. John Jacob Astor

_____ 2. Brigham Young

_____ 3. Daniel Boone

_____ 4. Santa Fe Trail

_____ 5. Zebulon Pike

_____ 6. Louisiana Purchase

_____ 7. Lewis and Clark expedition

_____ 8. Oregon Trail

_____ 9. Sacagawea

_____10. John C. Frémont

a. led an expedition to the Rocky Mountains in 1842 and wrote a report of his journey that became a guide for future travelers to the West

b. payment to France of $15 million, which roughly doubled the size of the United States

c. the route from Independence, Missouri, to Santa Fe, New Mexico

d. guide who was first to lead settlers beyond the Appalachians; cut a road west

e. Mormon leader who chose Utah as the group's new home

f. owner of the American Fur Company who founded the first important settlement in Oregon Country in 1811

g. Shoshone woman who helped the Lewis and Clark expedition by gathering edible fruits and vegetables for the group

h. the main route from the Mississippi River to the West Coast in the early 1800s

i. a long journey to explore the Louisiana Purchase

j. an explorer of the West who reached the summit of the mountain now known as Pike's Peak

MAIN IDEAS

1. Valuable deposits of gold and silver in the West created opportunities for wealth and brought more settlers to the region.
2. The cattle industry thrived on the Great Plains, supplying beef to the East.
3. The transcontinental railroad succeeded in linking the eastern and western United States.

Key Terms and People

frontier an area that is undeveloped

Comstock Lode name given to 1859 gold and silver discovery in western Nevada

boomtowns towns that serviced new mines and emptied when the mines closed

Cattle Kingdom the name given to the Great Plains during the years when they supported great herds of cattle

cattle drive movement of cattle herds to market or new grazing lands

Chisholm Trail a popular route for cattle drives from San Antonio to Abilene, Kansas

Pony Express mail delivery system in which messengers transported mail on horseback across the country

transcontinental railroad railroad across United States, connecting East and West

standard time system developed by railroad companies dividing the United States into four time zones

Lesson Summary

MINING BOOM BRINGS GROWTH

Around the time of the Civil War, most Americans thought of the Great Plains as the Great American Desert. After the Civil War, many Americans moved west. By 1850 the **frontier**, or undeveloped region, had reached the Pacific Ocean.

Settlers built homes and fenced off land. They started ranches and farms. Miners, ranchers, and farmers adapted to their new surroundings.

How would the environment in the frontier change as a result of the settlers?

____

____

____

In 1859 miners found gold and silver in western Nevada. News of the **Comstock Lode** (named after miner Henry Comstock) brought thousands to Nevada. Most miners could not afford the expensive equipment needed to remove gold and silver from quartz. They sold their claims to big businesses. Mining jobs were dangerous and low paying. Many immigrants came to work in the mines. As mines opened, **boomtowns** appeared. These were communities that grew suddenly. When the mines closed down, most boomtowns did too.

How did the discovery of precious metals affect Nevada's population?

____

____

THE CATTLE KINGDOM

Demand for beef in the East led to a booming cattle industry in Texas. Soon the cattle industry spread onto the Great Plains, creating a huge **Cattle Kingdom** with giant herds grazing the open range.

Cowboys cared for the cattle. They were responsible for the long **cattle drives** that got the cattle to Abilene, Kansas. There, the new railroad could ship the cattle to markets far away. The **Chisholm Trail** was one of these routes.

Underline the sentence that helps you to infer that cattle need large parcels of land for grazing.

THE TRANSCONTINENTAL RAILROAD

In 1860 the **Pony Express** improved communication between the East and the West. But it was replaced in 1861 by the telegraph, which could send messages much faster.

By 1862 Congress started passing laws that supported the building of a **transcontinental railroad**. By the end of 1863, the work had begun. One railroad line was building from the East and one from the West. In 1889 the two lines met at Promontory, Utah. Soon, railroads crisscrossed the country.

Based on what you have read, how would you define the word *transcontinental*?

____

____

____

Railroads provided better transportation for people and goods all over America. Rail travel also connected people in new ways. Before the railroads, each community determined its own time based on the sun. This caused problems for people who scheduled trains crossing a long distance. Railroad companies established **standard time**, dividing the United States into four time zones. By 1890 railroads were one of the nation's biggest industries.

CHALLENGE ACTIVITY

Critical Thinking: Evaluate Research the Pony Express to find out why it operated for only 18 months. Write an essay giving your opinion about whether the Pony Express was a success.

DIRECTIONS Look at each set of three vocabulary terms. On the line provided, write the letter of the term that does not relate to the others.

_____ 1. a. Cattle Kingdom
b. cattle drive
c. Pony Express

_____ 2. a. Comstock Lode
b. Chisholm Trail
c. cattle drive

_____ 3. a. boomtowns
b. frontier
c. Comstock Lode

_____ 4. a. cowboys
b. cattle drive
c. boomtowns

_____ 5. a. Pony Express
b. transcontinental railroad
c. standard time

_____ 6. a. transcontinental railroad
b. Pony Express
c. cowboys

_____ 7. a. cattle drive
b. Comstock Lode
c. open range

DIRECTIONS Read each sentence and fill in the blank with the word in the word pair that best completes the sentence.

8. Producing over $500 million worth of gold and silver, the ______________________ was a bonanza—a large deposit of precious ore. (Comstock Lode/frontier)

9. Often lasting several months and covering hundreds of miles, a ______________________________ was one of a cowboy's most important and dangerous duties. (open range/cattle drive)

10. Congress passed laws that supported the building of the ______________________________. (Pony Express/transcontinental railroad)

Lesson 3

MAIN IDEAS

1. As settlers moved to the Great Plains, they encountered the Plains Indians.
2. Native Americans attempted to keep their lands through treaties with the U.S. government.
3. Continued pressure from white settlement and government legislation brought the Plains Indians' traditional way of life to an end.

Key Terms and People

Treaty of Fort Laramie first major agreement signed with northern Plains nations

reservations areas of federal land set aside for Native Americans

Crazy Horse Sioux leader who violently protested reservations

Treaty of Medicine Lodge southern Plains Indians agreed to live on reservations

buffalo soldiers nickname given by Indians to African American cavalry

Sitting Bull Sioux leader who defeated Custer at Little Bighorn

George Armstrong Custer army commander who lost to the Sioux at Little Bighorn

Battle of the Little Bighorn last great victory for Sioux, where they defeated Custer

Massacre at Wounded Knee battle in which U.S. troops killed about 150 Sioux

Long Walk a 300-mile forced march of Navajo captives to a reservation

Chief Joseph Nez Percé chief who fled to Canada before being forced to a reservation

Geronimo Apache leader who continued to fight against the U.S. Army until 1886

Ghost Dance religious movement predicting a paradise for Native Americans

Sarah Winnemucca Paiute against the government's treatment of Native Americans

assimilate give up traditional ways and adopt the ways of a different group

Dawes General Allotment Act act that took almost 70 percent of reservation land

Lesson Summary

SETTLERS ENCOUNTER THE PLAINS INDIANS

As miners and settlers began crossing the Great Plains in the mid-1800s, they wanted access to more lands. The U.S. government tried to avoid disputes by negotiating the **Treaty of Fort Laramie**. It was the first major treaty between the U.S. government and the northern Plains Indians. Other treaties created **reservations** for Indians. Many refused to move. In 1866 **Crazy Horse** and his Sioux warriors killed 81 soldiers. By the 1867 **Treaty of Medicine Lodge**, most southern Plains Indians agreed to go to reservations.

What did settlers want that Indians had?

____

Why do you think that many Native Americans fought the move to reservations?

____

____

____

FIGHTING ON THE PLAINS

Native Americans of the northern Plains, Southwest, and Far West continued to resist reservations. The U.S. government sent **buffalo soldiers** and other troops to force Indians to leave.

In 1874 gold was discovered in the Black Hills of the Dakotas. The government wanted the Sioux to sell their reservation. **Sitting Bull** and other Sioux refused. In response, Lieutenant Colonel **George Armstrong Custer** ordered his soldiers to attack the Sioux. The Sioux won what became known as the **Battle of the Little Bighorn**. In the last great battle of the Plains Indians, 150 Sioux men, women, and children were killed in the **Massacre at Wounded Knee**.

Why did the government want the Sioux to sell their reservation?

____

____

____

Other Native Americans also fought forced removal. The Navajo tried to resist, but facing starvation, surrendered. They were led on a forced march to a reservation that became known as the **Long Walk**. Many died along the way.

Resistance also came from **Chief Joseph** and a group of Nez Percé, who wanted to keep their land in Oregon. In 1877 they fled across the border to Canada, but were captured by U.S.

How did Chief Joseph and the group he led resist relocating to a reservation?

____

____

troops and sent to a reservation. In 1886 Apache leader **Geronimo** and his warrior band surrendered, which ended Apache armed resistance.

A WAY OF LIFE ENDS

By the 1870s many Native Americans lived on reservations where land was not useful for farming or buffalo hunting. Many were starving. A Paiute leader named Wovoka started a religious movement, the **Ghost Dance**. It predicted paradise for Indians. But officials feared this movement would lead to rebellion. **Sarah Winnemucca**, another Paiute, called for reform of the reservation system.

Some reformers believed that Native Americans should **assimilate** by adopting the ways of white people. The **Dawes General Allotment Act** of 1887 took about two-thirds of Indian reservation land.

Why did officials worry about the spread of the Ghost Dance beliefs?

____

____

CHALLENGE ACTIVITY

Critical Thinking: Evaluate Choose a group of people: pioneers, miners, Sioux, soldiers. Write a paragraph describing how you think that group of people reacted to Custer's defeat.

Ghost Dance	Dawes General Allotment Act	reservations
buffalo soldiers	Battle of the Little Bighorn	Sarah Winnemucca
Chief Joseph	Long Walk	Sitting Bull
Crazy Horse	Massacre at Wounded Knee	Treaty of Fort Laramie

DIRECTIONS Read each sentence and chose a term from the word bank to fill in the blank.

1. ______________________ was a Sioux leader who defeated Custer at Little Bighorn.
2. The first major agreement signed with northern Plains nations was the ______________________.
3. ______________________ are areas of federal land set aside for Native Americans.
4. The nickname given by Indians to African American cavalry was ______________________.
5. The Navajos called a 300-mile forced march to a reservation the ______________________.
6. ______________________ called for reform of the reservation system.
7. The act that took back two-thirds of Indian land was the ______________________.
8. In the ______________________, the last great battle of the Plains Indians, 150 Sioux men, women, and children were killed.
9. A Paiute leader named Wovoka started a religious movement, the ______________________, that officials feared would lead to rebellion.
10. ______________________ and a group of Nez Percé wanted to keep their land in Oregon. They fled across the border to Canada before being forced to a reservation.

Westward Expansion

Lesson 4

MAIN IDEAS

1. Many Americans started new lives on the Great Plains.
2. Economic challenges led to the creation of farmers' political groups.
3. By the 1890s the western frontier had come to an end.

Key Terms and People

Homestead Act an 1862 act that gave government-owned land to farmers

Morrill Act an 1862 act that gave government-owned land to the states, with the understanding that the states would sell the land to finance colleges

Exodusters African Americans who left the South for Kansas in 1879

sodbusters nickname given to Great Plains farmers because breaking the soil was such hard work

dry farming farming using hardy crops that need less water than others

Annie Bidwell a Great Plains pioneer-reformer

deflation a decrease in the money supply and overall lower prices

National Grange a social and educational organization for farmers

William Jennings Bryan Democratic candidate for president in the 1888 election

Populist Party new national party formed by the country's farmers

Lesson Summary

NEW LIVES ON THE PLAINS

In 1862 two acts helped open the West to settlers. The **Homestead Act** gave government-owned land to small farmers. The **Morrill Act** granted millions of acres of government land to the states. The states would then sell that land and use the money to build colleges.

Underline the two congressional acts in 1862 that helped settle the West.

These acts attracted many groups to the Great Plains. This included single women who could get land through the Homestead Act. It also included up to 40,000 African Americans. Some called them **Exodusters** because of their exodus from the South. **Sodbusters** earned their nickname because breaking up the sod of the Great Plains was hard work. **Dry farming** helped

How did sodbusters get their nickname?

____

____

____

the sodbusters succeed. In addition, the steel plow developed by John Deere, the windmill, barbed wire, and mechanical reapers and threshers all made farmwork more efficient.

Circle the inventions that made farming the Plains more efficient.

Some pioneer women, such as author Laura Ingalls Wilder and suffragist **Annie Bidwell**, became famous. Most settlers lived a lonely life, though. They were isolated on the remote farms of the Plains. Early farmers also had to build their own communities.

FARMERS' POLITICAL GROUPS

Modern machines made farming more productive. This productivity, however, led to overproduction, which in turn led to lower crop prices. To make matters worse, at this time the U.S. economy was affected by **deflation**, in which the money supply decreased and prices dropped. So although farmers farmed more, they made less money for their crops. Many lost their farms during this time.

Why could banding together help farmers?

____

____

____

To help each other, farmers formed the **National Grange** (*grange* is an old word for "granary"). The Grange worked to better farmers' lives. It worked to get the railroads regulated. It also backed political candidates such as **William Jennings Bryan**.

In 1892 political organizations called Farmers' Alliances formed a new pro-farmer political party. They called it the **Populist Party**. In the 1896 presidential elections, it supported Democrat Bryan. Bryan lost and the Populist Party dissolved.

Why do you think the Populist Party dissolved after Bryan lost the presidential election?

____

____

____

END OF THE FRONTIER

In 1889 the government opened Oklahoma to homesteaders. These pioneers quickly claimed more than 11 million acres of land. The frontier existed no more.

What ended America's frontier?

____

____

CHALLENGE ACTIVITY

Critical Thinking: Analyze Tell why overproduction on farms could lead to lower prices for crops.

DIRECTIONS Read each sentence and fill in the blank with the word in the word pair that best completes the sentence.

1. _______________________ emphasized the planting of hardy crops that need less water than other crops. (Exodusters/Dry farming)

2. _________________________ was a political candidate for the Populist Party. (William Jennings Bryan/John Deere)

3. The states were granted millions of acres of federal land through the _________________________. (Morrill Act/National Grange)

4. The _________________________ was a social and educational organization that sought to improve the quality of life for farmers and their families. (Morrill Act/National Grange)

5. ______________________ earned their nickname because of the hard work needed to break up the sod of the Great Plains. (Sodbusters/Exodusters)

6. _______________________ was a well-known pioneer woman who supported a number of moral and social causes, including the women's suffrage movement. (Laura Ingalls Wilder/Annie Bidwell)

7. Political organizations called Farmers' Alliances formed the new national pro-farmer _________________________. (Populist Party/Sodbusters)

8. Through the ______________________, passed by Congress in 1862, individual citizens could receive land. (Homestead Act/Morrill Act)

9. ______________________ were those African Americans who left the South in the late nineteenth century, seeking land in Kansas being offered by the federal government under the Homestead Act. (Exodusters/National Grange)

Name ______________________ Class ______________ Date __________

Expansion and Conflict

Lesson 1

MAIN IDEAS

1. Many American settlers moved to Texas after Mexico achieved independence from Spain.
2. Texans revolted against Mexican rule and established an independent nation.

Key Terms and People

Father Miguel Hidalgo y Costilla priest who led the first major Mexican revolt against Spanish rule in 1810

empresarios agents of the Mexican republic hired to bring settlers to Texas

Stephen F. Austin empresario who established the first American colony in Texas

Antonio López de Santa Anna Mexican leader who came to power in 1830 and suspended Mexico's constitution

Alamo an old mission in San Antonio occupied by Texan revolutionary forces in 1836

Battle of San Jacinto decisive victory that gave Texas independence from Mexico

Lesson Summary

AMERICAN SETTLERS MOVE TO TEXAS

In the early 1800s, the region we know as the American Southwest was part of Mexico. Mexico was part of the vast Spanish empire. Mexico struggled against Spanish rule. A revolt led by **Father Miguel Hidalgo y Costilla** in 1810 failed, but the rebellion he started grew. In 1821 Mexico became independent.

During the early 1800s, what empire did California and Texas belong to?

____

The new Mexican republic hired agents known as **empresarios** to bring settlers there. One of these, **Stephen F. Austin**, selected a site on the lower Colorado River. There he settled 300 families, mostly from the southern states. These settlers often ignored Mexican laws, including the law forbidding slavery.

From what region of the United States did most settlers come to Texas?

____

Tension grew between Mexico's central government and the American settlers. Colonists were angry when **Antonio López de Santa Anna** came to power in 1830 and suspended Mexico's constitution. Austin was imprisoned for a year and a half. When he returned to Texas, he began urging Texans to rebel against Mexico.

Underline the sentence that helps explain why tension grew between the central Mexican government and the American settlers in Texas.

TEXANS REVOLT AGAINST MEXICO

Hostilities began with a battle at Gonzalez in 1835. Santa Anna inflicted two brutal defeats on the Texans at the **Alamo** and Goliad. However, Texas forces under Sam Houston won a decisive victory over Santa Anna at the **Battle of San Jacinto**. Santa Anna signed a treaty giving Texas its independence.

Most people in the new Republic of Texas hoped that Texas would join the United States. However, U.S. president Andrew Jackson was concerned about two factors. He was worried that admitting Texas as a slave state would upset the balance between free and slave states. Also, Jackson feared that annexing Texas might lead to a war with Mexico.

What was Texas called after the treaty was signed?

____

____

As the annexation of Texas was delayed, more American settlers came from nearby southern states. They often brought slaves with them to work the land and to grow cotton. Tensions between the people of Mexico and Texas remained high. After a few unsettled years, Texas president Sam Houston signed a peace treaty with Mexico in 1844.

What did many American settlers bring with them to Texas?

____

____

CHALLENGE ACTIVITY

Critical Thinking: Evaluate Take sides in a debate as to whether Texas should join the United States or remain an independent nation. Write an explicit defense of your position.

Alamo	Stephen F. Austin	Battle of San Jacinto
empresarios	Father Miguel Hidalgo y Costilla	Republic of Texas
	Antonio López de Santa Anna	

DIRECTIONS Write two adjectives or descriptive phrases that describe the term given.

1. empresarios ____

   ____

2. Stephen F. Austin ____

   ____

3. Antonio López de Santa Anna ____

   ____

4. Alamo ____

   ____

5. Battle of San Jacinto ____

   ____

DIRECTIONS Read each sentence and fill in the blank with the word in the word pair that best completes the sentence.

6. In 1820 ______________________ led a rebellion of about 80,000 poor American Indians and mestizos hoping to win Mexico's independence from Spain. (Antonio López de Santa Anna/Father Miguel Hidalgo y Costilla)
7. ______________________ was one of the empresarios who brought settlers to Texas. (Stephen F. Austin/Sam Houston)
8. Sam Houston's Texas army defeated ______________________ at the ______________________. (Antonio López de Santa Anna/ Father Miguel Hidalgo y Costilla); (Alamo/Battle of San Jacinto)
9. The independent nation of Texas was called the ______________. (Alamo/Republic of Texas)

Lesson 2

MAIN IDEAS

1. Many Americans believed that the nation had a manifest destiny to claim new lands in the West.
2. As a result of the Mexican-American War, the United States added territory in the Southwest.
3. American settlement in the Mexican Cession produced conflict and a blending of cultures.

Key Terms and People

manifest destiny belief that America's fate was to conquer land all the way to the Pacific Ocean

James K. Polk U.S. president, elected in 1844, whose administration annexed both Texas and Oregon

vaqueros cowboys

Californios Spanish colonists and their descendants living in California

Bear Flag Revolt rebellion of American settlers against the Californios in 1846

Treaty of Guadalupe Hidalgo 1848 peace treaty between Mexico and the United States

Gadsden Purchase purchase from Mexico of the southern parts of present-day New Mexico and Arizona in 1853

Lesson Summary

MANIFEST DESTINY

The idea of **manifest destiny** affected the election of 1844. The new president, **James K. Polk**, promised to annex both Texas and Oregon. In 1846 Britain and the United States signed a treaty. Oregon south of the 49th parallel would belong to the United States. This treaty drew the present-day border between the United States and Canada. In 1845 the congresses of both the Republic of Texas and the U.S. approved annexation of Texas.

How did the boundaries of the United States change during the 1840s?

____

____

After winning independence in 1821, Mexico began changing old policies set by Spain. Mission lands were broken up into ranches. ***Vaqueros*** managed the herds of cattle and sheep. Settlers, known as **Californios**, felt little connection to their faraway government in Mexico. American settlers coming to California called for independence from Mexico.

How might Californios have viewed the arrival of large numbers of American settlers?

____

____

____

MEXICAN-AMERICAN WAR

Since the Texas Revolution, the border between Mexico and Texas had been in dispute. Mexico claimed the border lay along the Nueces River. The United States claimed the Rio Grande as the border. In 1845 President Polk sent troops to the Rio Grande. When Mexican soldiers attacked them, Congress declared war on Mexico. Although many Americans thought the war was unjustified, U.S. troops pushed into Mexico. Finally they captured Mexico City. A successful revolt against the Californios in Sonoma, known as the **Bear Flag Revolt**, proclaimed California to be an independent nation.

Some Americans at the time thought President Polk provoked the Mexican attack by stationing soldiers on the Rio Grande. Do you agree? Explain your answer.

____

____

____

AMERICAN SETTLEMENT IN THE MEXICAN CESSION

The **Treaty of Guadalupe Hidalgo** ended the Mexican War in 1848. The agreement increased the land area of the United States by almost 25 percent. In 1853 the **Gadsden Purchase** fixed the continental boundaries of the United States.

As American settlers flooded the Southwest, the elements of life changed. Cultural encounters often led to conflict and violence. New settlers usually ignored Mexican legal ideas, such as community property and water rights. However, gradually people began to share ideas and trade improved.

Why is the issue of water rights much more serious in the West than it is in the East?

____

____

____

CHALLENGE ACTIVITY

Critical Thinking: Identify Cause and Effect Write a law regulating water rights.

DIRECTIONS Read each sentence and fill in the blank with the word in the word pair that best completes the sentence.

1. The ______________________ was negotiated with Mexico so that the United States government would pay Mexico for the southern parts of what are now Arizona and New Mexico. (Gadsden Purchase/Bear Flag Revolt)
2. The growth of the United States to the Pacific Ocean was called ______________________. (Californios/manifest destiny)
3. In Mexico, ______________________ managed the herds of cattle and sheep. (*vaqueros*/Californios)
4. The Mexican-American War ended with the signing of the ______________ __________________. (manifest destiny/Treaty of Guadalupe Hidalgo)
5. Spanish colonists in California were known as ______________________. (Californios/*vaqueros*)
6. The rebellion in 1846 was called the ______________________ because of the flag that was created to represent the nation of California. (Bear Flag Revolt/Gadsden Purchase)
7. ______________________ was elected president of the United States in 1844. (Henry Clay/James K. Polk)
8. The ______________________ finally fixed the continental boundaries of the United States. (Bear Flag Revolt/Gadsden Purchase)

Lesson 3

MAIN IDEAS

1. The discovery of gold brought settlers to California.
2. The gold rush had a lasting impact on California's population and economy.

Key Terms and People

John Sutter Swiss immigrant who started the first Anglo-Californian colony in 1839

Donner party a group of western travelers who were trapped crossing the Sierra Nevada mountains in the winter of 1846–47

forty-niners gold-seeking migrants who traveled to California in 1849

placer miners miners who used pans or other devices to wash gold nuggets from loose rock or gravel

prospect search for gold

Lesson Summary

DISCOVERY OF GOLD BRINGS SETTLERS

Before 1840 few Americans settled in California. However, there was trade between Mexico and the United States. After Mexico allowed **John Sutter** to establish a colony in 1839, many more American settlers began arriving. In one tragic incident, heavy snows in the Sierra Nevada mountains trapped a group of travelers known as the **Donner party**. Half of the travelers died. They froze or starved to death.

What country was California part of in 1840?

____

Gold was discovered at Sutter's Mill in 1848. The news spread across the country. During 1849 about 80,000 **forty-niners** came to California hoping to strike it rich. Most of them arrived in the small port town of San Francisco. The population of San Francisco grew from around 800 to more than 25,000.

Would mining experience have helped the average forty-niner? Explain your answer.

____

____

____

Mining methods varied. **Placer miners** would **prospect** by using pans to wash gold nuggets out of the loose rock and gravel. Richer miners established companies to dig shafts and tunnels. Many success stories inspired prospectors. However, the good luck that made some miners wealthy never came to thousands of gold seekers. All they found was misery and debt.

Mining camps sprang up. Among the gold seekers were immigrants from Mexico, China, Europe, and South America. Many found they could earn a living by supplying miners with basic services like cooking or washing clothes. One example is Biddy Mason. She and her family were slaves brought by a forty-niner from Georgia. They gained their freedom and managed to buy some land near the village of Los Angeles. Soon, Mason became one of the wealthiest landowners in California.

Who had more "job security," the miners or the service providers? Why?

____

____

____

IMPACT ON CALIFORNIA

The forty-niners brought a population explosion and an economic boom to California. It became the thirty-first state of the Union in 1850. As the gold rush faded, many Californians took to farming and ranching. However, California remained isolated from the rest of the country until the transcontinental railroad was completed in 1869.

What consequence of the gold rush made California eligible for statehood?

____

____

____

CHALLENGE ACTIVITY

Critical Thinking: Make Inferences Design and write a brochure inviting easterners to come to Sutter's colony in California and start a new life.

Biddy Mason	forty-niners	prospect	Sutter's Mill
Donner party	John Sutter	placer miners	

DIRECTIONS Write two adjectives or descriptive phrases that describe the term.

1. forty-niners ______________________________

____

2. prospect ______________________________

____

3. placer miners ______________________________

____

DIRECTIONS On the line provided before each statement, write **T** if a statement is true and **F** if a statement is false. If the statement is false, write the correct term on the line after each sentence that makes the sentence a true statement.

_____ 4. Biddy Mason arrived in California as a slave, but gained freedom and became one of the wealthiest landowners in California, a community leader, and a well-known supporter of charities.

____

_____ 5. Swiss immigrant John Sutter was given permission by Mexican officials to start a colony in California.

____

_____ 6. The Donner party was a group of western travelers who became lost in the Sierra Nevada.

____

_____ 7. When it was learned that gold was discovered near Biddy Mason, the California gold rush began.

____

Name ____________________ Class ______________ Date __________

The North

Lesson 1

MAIN IDEAS

1. The invention of new machines in Great Britain led to the beginning of the Industrial Revolution.
2. The development of new machines and processes brought the Industrial Revolution to the United States.
3. Despite a slow start in manufacturing, the United States made rapid improvements during the War of 1812.

Key Terms and People

Industrial Revolution a period of rapid growth in the use of machines in manufacturing and production

textiles cloth items

Richard Arkwright an inventor who patented a large spinning machine, called the water frame, that ran on water power and created dozens of cotton threads at once

Samuel Slater a skilled British mechanic who could build better textile machines

technology the tools used to produce items or to do work

Eli Whitney an inventor with an idea for mass-producing guns

interchangeable parts parts of a machine that are exactly the same

mass production the efficient production of large numbers of identical goods

Lesson Summary

THE INDUSTRIAL REVOLUTION

In the early 1700s, most people in the United States and Europe made a living by farming. Female family members often used hand tools to make cloth for families. The sale of extra cloth earned money. Skilled workers such as blacksmiths set up shops to earn money by manufacturing goods by hand.

In what way were goods made in the early 1700s?

____

The **Industrial Revolution** would completely change that way of life. By the mid-1700s, cities and populations had grown. Demand increased for efficient and faster ways to make items.

A new way of making **textiles** provided the first breakthrough. **Richard Arkwright** invented a machine that lowered the cost of cotton cloth and raised production speed. The machine was large and needed a power source. Most textile mills were built near streams to use running water for power.

In what way did Arkwright's machine make history?

____

____

NEW MACHINES AND PROCESSES

Samuel Slater knew how to build machines that were used in Britain to make cloth more efficiently. He emigrated to the United States and opened a mill in Pawtucket, Rhode Island, with Moses Brown. The mill made cotton thread by machine. It was a success. Most mills were in the Northeast, a region with many rivers and streams for power.

What information did Slater bring with him to the United States?

____

____

____

In the 1790s U.S. gunmakers could not produce muskets quickly enough to satisfy the government's demand. Better **technology** was needed. **Eli Whitney** had the idea of manufacturing using **interchangeable parts**. Whitney assembled muskets for President John Adams. Whitney's ideas helped speed up **mass production** of goods for the marketplace.

What was Whitney's revolutionary idea?

____

____

____

MANUFACTURING GROWS SLOWLY

U.S. manufacturing spread slowly. People who could buy good farmland would not work for low factory wages. British goods were cheaper than American goods. However, during the War of 1812, many Americans learned that they had relied on foreign goods too much. In 1815 the war ended and free trade returned. Business-people wanted to lead the nation into a time of industrial growth.

Why did American manufacturing spread slowly?

____

____

CHALLENGE ACTIVITY

Critical Thinking: Rank Compare the three inventors in this lesson. Rank them 1 to 3, where 1 is the person you think had the biggest impact on manufacturing in America. Defend your ranking in a brief essay.

Eli Whitney	Industrial Revolution	interchangeable parts
mass production	Richard Arkwright	Samuel Slater
technology	textiles	

DIRECTIONS Read each sentence and fill in the blank with the word in the word pair that best completes the sentence.

1. The ______________________________ was a period of rapid growth in the use of machines in manufacturing and production. (interchangeable parts/ Industrial Revolution)
2. The efficient production of large numbers of identical goods is called ______________________________. (mass production/Industrial Revolution)
3. Products with ______________________________ are made from pieces that are exactly the same. (interchangeable parts/textiles)
4. British entrepreneur ______________________________ invented a large spinning machine, called the water frame, that ran on water power. (Samuel Slater/Richard Arkwright)
5. ______________________________ was a skilled British mechanic who knew how to build better textile machines. (Samuel Slater/Richard Arkwright)
6. The tools used to produce items or to do work are called ______________________________. (textiles/technology)
7. Inventor ______________________________ came up with the idea of using interchangeable parts. (Samuel Slater/Eli Whitney)
8. The first important breakthrough of the Industrial Revolution took place in how ______________________________, or cloth items, were made. (textiles/technology)

The North

Lesson 2

MAIN IDEAS

1. The spread of mills in the Northeast changed workers' lives.
2. The Lowell system revolutionized the textile industry in the Northeast.
3. Workers organized to reform working conditions.

Key Terms and People

Rhode Island system Samuel Slater's strategy of hiring families and dividing factory work into simple tasks

Francis Cabot Lowell New England entrepreneur whose ideas completely changed the textile industry in the Northeast

Lowell system Lowell's practice of hiring young unmarried women to work in his mills

trade unions groups of skilled workers that tried to improve members' pay and working conditions

strikes union workers' refusal to work until their employers met their demands

Sarah G. Bagley a mill worker who founded the Lowell Female Labor Reform Association

Lesson Summary

MILLS CHANGE WORKERS' LIVES

Samuel Slater had difficulty hiring enough people to work in his mills. Young male apprentices often left because they thought their work was boring. Slater began hiring entire families to move to Pawtucket.

Slater constructed housing for the workers. He paid workers in credit at the company store rather than paying them cash. This way Slater could reinvest money in his business. Children usually earned in one week what an adult was paid for one day's work. Slater's method was known as the **Rhode Island system**. Many northeastern mill owners imitated Slater's system.

How much did child workers earn in factories?

____

____

THE LOWELL SYSTEM

Francis Cabot Lowell developed a different approach called the **Lowell system**. It transformed the Northeast's textile industry. With the aid of a company, Lowell built mills in Waltham and Lowell, both in Massachusetts. The factories were clean, and the workers' boardinghouses were neat.

Many young women, called Lowell girls, journeyed from across New England to earn money instead of working on the family farm. The Lowell girls were encouraged to take classes and join clubs. However, they worked 12- to 14-hour days, and cotton dust caused health problems for them.

Name one advantage and one disadvantage of Lowell mill work.

____

____

____

WORKERS ORGANIZE

Factory workers' wages went down as people competed for jobs. Many immigrants entered the workplace, causing even more competition. The Panic of 1837 led to unemployment for many. Skilled workers started **trade unions** for protection. Sometimes union members held strikes. But most **strikes** were not very successful.

Sarah G. Bagley battled for the workers. She was the first woman to hold a high-ranking position in America's labor movement. In 1840 President Martin Van Buren had given a ten-hour workday to many federal employees. Bagley wanted the ten-hour workday for all workers.

The unions won some legal victories. Some states passed ten-hour workday laws. But companies often found ways to get around them. Other states did not pass the ten-hour workday laws. Union supporters kept fighting for improved working conditions during the 1800s.

Why did workers' pay decrease?

____

____

What did workers achieve in the mid-1800s?

____

____

CHALLENGE ACTIVITY

Critical Thinking: Contrast Write a letter to the editor contrasting the lives of workers in Slater's mills and Lowell's mills.

Sarah G. Bagley	Francis Cabot Lowell	Lowell system
Rhode Island system	strikes	trade unions

DIRECTIONS On the line provided before each statement, write **T** if a statement is true and **F** if a statement is false. If the statement is false, write the correct term on the line after each sentence that makes the sentence a true statement.

_____ 1. The Lowell system included practices such as hiring young unmarried women from local farms to work in the textile mill.

____

_____ 2. Sometimes union members staged protests called trade unions.

____

_____ 3. The Lowell system was Samuel Slater's strategy of hiring families and dividing factory work into simple tasks.

____

_____ 4. One of the strongest female voices in the union movement belonged to Sarah G. Bagley, who founded the Lowell Female Labor Reform Association.

____

_____ 5. Francis Cabot Lowell was a businessman from New England whose ideas completely changed the textile industry in the Northest.

____

______ 6. Groups that tried to improve pay and working conditions for their members were called strikes.

____

______ 7. Mill owners advertised for "Men with growing families wanted" in support of the Lowell system.

____

______ 8. Workers on strike refuse to work until their employers meet their demands.

____

Lesson 3

MAIN IDEAS

1. The Transportation Revolution affected trade and daily life.
2. The steamboat was one of the first developments of the Transportation Revolution.
3. Railroads were a vital part of the Transportation Revolution.
4. The Transportation Revolution brought many changes to American life and industry.

Key Terms and People

Transportation Revolution a period of rapid growth in the speed and convenience of travel

Robert Fulton an American inventor who tested the first full-sized commercial steamboat in the United States

Clermont a steamboat that could travel up the Hudson River with no trouble

Gibbons* v. *Ogden Supreme Court ruling that said the federal government had authority to regulate trade between states

Peter Cooper an American who built the *Tom Thumb*, a small, steam-powered railroad locomotive with great power and speed

Lesson Summary

TRADE AND DAILY LIFE

Along with the Industrial Revolution, the **Transportation Revolution** changed life in the 1800s. This happened through the growth in the speed of travel and the decreasing cost of shipping goods. People and information began traveling at much higher speeds. New towns and businesses sprang up. Communication, travel, and trade improved. The steamboat and the railroad, new kinds of transportation, quickened the pace of American life.

Why did information begin traveling at higher speeds?

____

____

____

In what way might the pace of American life have increased?

____

____

____

STEAMBOATS

American and European inventors had developed steam-powered boats in the late 1700s. In 1807 American steamboat designer **Robert Fulton** tested the ***Clermont***, the first full-sized commercial steamboat, on the Hudson River. The successful test helped to launch the steamboat era.

Steamboats were well-suited to river travel. They could move upriver and did not rely on wind power. Steamboats and the location of rivers in the United States created new economic opportunities during the 1800s. By the 1850s steamboats were also being used to carry people and goods across the Atlantic Ocean, creating international trade.

How did steamboats affect shipping?

____

____

____

Sometimes the changes in transportation led to legal conflicts. In the landmark case ***Gibbons* v. *Ogden***, the court ruled that federal shipping laws overruled state shipping laws. The ruling freed up waters to even greater trade and competition within the shipping industry.

AMERICAN RAILROADS

In 1830 **Peter Cooper** built the *Tom Thumb*, a small but powerful train locomotive. He raced the locomotive against a horse-drawn railcar.

Excitement over rail travel grew in the mid-1800s. By 1860 about 30,000 miles of railroad tracks joined nearly every major eastern U.S. city. Trains took goods to faraway markets. Train travel averaged about 20 miles per hour. It could be dangerous because of fires and derailment. But the dangers did not discourage travelers who wanted to go places faster.

Underline the sentence that explains why travelers put up with the dangers of railroad travel.

TRANSPORTATION REVOLUTION BRINGS CHANGES

Trains brought new residents and raw materials for industry to cities, spurring growth. Coal replaced wood as a source of fuel because it was cheaper and produced more energy. That led to growth in the coal-mining industry. Steel was used for railroad tracks, so the demand for steel increased. Railroad transportation also helped logging expand because wood was needed to

What caused growth in the steel industry?

____

____

____

build new houses in the growing cities. Chicago, on Lake Michigan, became a hub for national transportation.

CHALLENGE ACTIVITY

Critical Thinking: Design Design a four-page brochure advertising the wonders of travel by steamboat or train.

DIRECTIONS Write two adjectives or descriptive phrases that describe the term.

1. *Clermont* ____

   ____

2. *Gibbons* v. *Ogden* ____

   ____

3. Peter Cooper ____

   ____

4. Robert Fulton ____

   ____

5. Transportation Revolution ____

   ____

DIRECTIONS Look at each set of four vocabulary terms following each number. On the line provided, write the letter of the term that does not relate to the others.

_____	6. a. *Clermont*	b. Robert Fulton	c. *Tom Thumb*	d. steamboat
_____	7. a. *Tom Thumb*	b. steamboat	c. Peter Cooper	d. locomotive
_____	8. a. coal	b. steel	c. fuel	d. wood

DIRECTIONS Read each sentence and fill in the blank with the word in the word pair that best completes the sentence.

9. The Supreme Court ruled in the case of ______________________________ that federal law overruled state law. (*Tom Thumb*/*Gibbons* v. *Ogden*)
10. During the Transportation Revolution, ______________________________ replaced wood as the main source of power. (steel/coal)
11. ______________________________ designed the first full-sized commercial steamboat, called the ______________________________, in the United States. (Peter Cooper/Robert Fulton); (*Clermont*/*Tom Thumb*)
12. The locomotive ______________________________, built by ______________________________, caused interest in railroads in the United States. (*Clermont*/*Tom Thumb*); (Peter Cooper/Robert Fulton)
13. A period of rapid growth in the speed and convenience of travel is called the ______________________________. (Transportation Revolution/Industrial Revolution)

Name ______________________ Class ________________ Date __________

Lesson 4

MAIN IDEAS

1. The telegraph made swift communication possible from coast to coast.
2. With the shift to steam power, businesses built factories closer to cities and transportation centers.
3. Improved farm equipment and other labor-saving devices made life easier for many Americans.
4. New inventions changed lives in American homes.

Key Terms and People

Samuel F. B. Morse the inventor of the telegraph

telegraph a device that could send information over wires across great distances

Morse code a system in which dots and dashes are used to stand for each letter of the alphabet

John Deere a blacksmith who created the steel plow design

Cyrus McCormick the developer of a new harvesting machine called a mechanical reaper

Isaac Singer an inventor who made improvements in the design of the sewing machine

Lesson Summary

TELEGRAPH SPEEDS COMMUNICATION

Samuel F. B. Morse invented the **telegraph** in 1832. Morse used the work of other scientists in making this practical machine. Telegraphs carry pulses of electric current over wires. The operator touches a bar that sets the length of each pulse. At the wire's other end, the pulses change into clicks. A short click is a dot. A long click is a dash.

What was the invention of the telegraph based on?

____

____

Morse's partner, Alfred Lewis Vail, developed the **Morse code**. Some people did not think Morse could actually read messages sent across long distances. But during the 1844 Democratic Convention in Baltimore, Maryland, a telegraph wired news of a nomination to politicians who were in Washington. Soon telegraphs were relaying messages for businesses, the government,

Did everyone accept the telegraph's power at first?

____

____

newspapers, and private citizens. Telegraph lines were strung on poles next to railroad tracks across the country.

Why did telegraph messages become so widely used?

____

____

____

STEAM POWER AND NEW FACTORIES

Most factories, operating on water power at first, had to be built near water. With the use of steam engines, factories could be built almost anywhere. Still, most were in the Northeast. By 1860 New England had as many factories as the entire South had. Many new factories were near cities and transportation centers, giving them better access to workers. In addition, by the 1840s new machinery could produce interchangeable parts.

Why could newer factories be built almost anywhere?

____

____

____

IMPROVED FARM EQUIPMENT

John Deere was selling 1,000 steel plows a year by 1846. **Cyrus McCormick** mass-produced his reapers in a large Chicago factory. His company advertised, provided service, and let customers buy on credit. The plow and the reaper allowed Midwestern farmers to harvest huge crop fields.

Underline the sentence that explains what new methods McCormick used to persuade people to buy his reapers.

CHANGING LIFE AT HOME

The sewing machine was among the American inventions that made home life easier. **Isaac Singer** modified the sewing machine and worked hard to sell his product. Prices of many household items had decreased, giving many more people the ability to afford them.

Why did the purchase of many household items increase?

____

____

CHALLENGE ACTIVITY

Critical Thinking: Evaluate Write a brief essay explaining which invention mentioned in this section made the biggest change in people's lives.

John Deere	Cyrus McCormick	Samuel F. B. Morse
Morse code	Isaac Singer	telegraph

DIRECTIONS Match the names in the first column with the invention or development with which they are associated from the second column by placing the letter of the correct definition in the space provided before each name.

_____ 1. Samuel F. B. Morse

_____ 2. John Deere

_____ 3. Isaac Singer

_____ 4. Cyrus McCormick

_____ 5. Alfred Lewis Vail

a. developed the mechanical reaper

b. improved and marketed the sewing machine

c. developed Morse code

d. perfected the telegraph

e. designed a steel plow

DIRECTIONS Choose five of the vocabulary words from the word list. Use these words to write a summary of what you learned in the section.

____

____

____

____

____

____

____

____

____

____

____

____

Name ______________________________ Class __________________ Date ___________

The South

Lesson 1

MAIN IDEAS

1. The invention of the cotton gin revived the economy of the South.
2. The cotton gin created a cotton boom in which farmers grew little else.
3. Some people encouraged southerners to focus on other crops and industries.

Key Terms and People

cotton gin machine that removes seeds from cotton

planters large-scale farmers who owned more than 20 slaves

cotton belt nickname for the region that grew most of the country's cotton crop

factors crop brokers who arranged transportation of goods aboard trading ships

Tredegar Iron Works one of the most productive iron works in the nation; the only large southern factory that made iron products

Lesson Summary

REVIVING THE SOUTH'S ECONOMY

The use of slaves began to decline after the American Revolution. Because crop prices fell, farmers planted less. So they needed less slave labor.

Why was it difficult to harvest cotton before the invention of the cotton gin?

____

____

Cotton was not a new crop to the southern states. However, few farmers planted much cotton. That is because the short-staple cotton that grew well there was very hard to separate from its seeds. Northerner Eli Whitney changed that when he invented the **cotton gin**.

This hand-cranked cylinder had wire teeth that easily pulled cotton fibers and seeds apart. With the cotton gin, cotton crops became profitable. A cotton gin could clean as much cotton as planters could plant and their slaves could pick. A **planter** was a large-scale farmer who owned more than 20 slaves.

THE COTTON BOOM

For southern farmers, cotton had many advantages as a cash crop over other crops. Unlike food products, cotton could be stored for long periods of time. Plus its lightness made it fairly inexpensive to transport. As a result, the cotton-supported slave trade grew, even as Congress worked to limit slavery in the nation.

What were the advantages of cotton compared to other crops?

____

____

____

Most of the country's cotton was produced in the **cotton belt**. This stretched from South Carolina to Texas. Without transportation systems such as roads and canals, southern farmers relied on rivers to move their cotton. When the cotton reached a port, the farmers sold their cotton to merchants. They then contacted **factors** to arrange transportation for the cotton aboard trading ships.

Why were the region's rivers especially important to southern farmers?

____

____

____

OTHER CROPS AND INDUSTRIES

Scientific agriculture, or the use of scientific methods to improve farming, encouraged southern farmers to rotate the kinds of crops they planted. The primary food crop of the South was corn. However, farmers also grew rice, sugarcane, wheat, tobacco, hemp, and flax. Some southerners encouraged the growth of industry. As a result, some industries, such as the **Tredegar Iron Works** owned by Joseph R. Anderson in Richmond, Virginia, also flourished, producing bridge materials, cannons, steam engines, and other products. Still, most of the South focused on farming.

Underline the definition of *scientific agriculture*.

CHALLENGE ACTIVITY

Critical Thinking: Explain What if a new fiber was discovered that replaced cotton in clothing? What effect would this development have on cotton planters? Write a paragraph explaining how falling cotton prices might lead to less demand for farmworkers.

DIRECTIONS Look at each set of four vocabulary terms. On the line provided, write the letter of the term that does not relate to the others.

_____ 1. a. Eli Whitney
b. cotton gin
c. Joseph R. Anderson
d. planters

_____ 2. a. Joseph R. Anderson
b. planters
c. Tredegar Iron Works
d. industry

_____ 3. a. scientific agriculture
b. cotton belt
c. factors
d. Tredegar Iron Works

_____ 4. a. Joseph R. Anderson
b. cotton belt
c. planters
d. cotton gin

_____ 5. a. factors
b. Eli Whitney
c. Tredegar Iron Works
d. scientific agriculture

DIRECTIONS Read each sentence and fill in the blank with the word in the word pair that best completes the sentence.

6. The ______________________________ was a simple device that used a hand-cranked cylinder with wire teeth to pull cotton fibers apart from the seeds. (cotton gin/cotton belt)
7. ______________________________ were large-scale farmers who held more than 20 slaves. (Planters/Factors)
8. The region that stretched from South Carolina to Texas became known as the ______________________________, because it was the area that grew most of the country's cotton. (cotton gin/cotton belt)
9. The ______________________________ in Richmond, Virginia, produced bridge materials, cannons, steam engines, and other products. (Eli Whitney/Tredegar Iron Works)
10. Crop brokers called ______________________________ managed the cotton trade in port cities. (planters/factors)

Lesson 2

MAIN IDEAS

1. Southern society and culture consisted of four main groups.
2. Free African Americans in the South faced a great deal of discrimination.

Key Terms and People

yeomen owners of small farms

Lesson Summary

SOUTHERN SOCIETY AND CULTURE

Only about one-third of all southerners owned slaves. Far fewer were actually wealthy planters. However, those few planters were among the most influential southern citizens, and many were political leaders.

On the vast plantations, the planter ran the farm business. A wealthy planter would have overseers to help him. The planter's wife ran the household, which included many house slaves. She also was in charge of important social events such as dances and dinners.

Most southern farmers were yeomen. **Yeomen** owned small farms averaging about 100 acres, and often they worked side by side with the few slaves they might own.

How was a yeoman different from a planter?

____
____
____

Many white southerners were poor. They owned no slaves at all. Often they lived on land that could not grow crops. These farmers were at the bottom of the economic ladder.

Religion was central to southern life. One reason was its social impact. Often farm families saw their neighbors only at church functions. Some southerners also believed that Christianity justified slavery—a belief not shared by Christians in the North.

Why was religion central to southern life?

____
____
____

The economy of the South also depended on the businesses conducted in its busy cities. As in northern cities, southern cities provided many services to residents, including water systems and street maintenance. Southern cities used slave labor, too. Businesses either owned slaves or hired them out from nearby planters.

How were southern cities like northern cities?

____

____

____

FREE AFRICAN AMERICANS AND DISCRIMINATION

Not all African Americans in the South were slaves. Some were free. Some had been born free. Others had bought their freedom from their slave owners or had run away. More than 250,000 free African Americans lived in the South by 1860. Most lived in the countryside and worked as paid laborers on plantations and farms. Free African Americans who lived in cities worked in a variety of jobs, mostly as skilled artisans.

Underline the sentence describing how many free African Americans lived in the South.

Southern states passed laws that limited the rights of free African Americans. For example, in some places they could not vote or hold certain jobs. They were not allowed to live where they chose or travel freely. This discrimination existed because some southerners were concerned about the presence of free African Americans. They worried that those who were free would incite those who were enslaved to rise up against slaveholders. They believed that free African Americans posed a threat to the institution of slavery.

According to many southerners, how did free African Americans threaten the South's slave system?

____

____

____

Some southerners believed that free African Americans could not survive outside of slavery. They used this as justification for slavery. However, if free African Americans could support themselves, then southern thinking could be proved wrong.

CHALLENGE ACTIVITY

Critical Thinking: Evaluate How effective were the laws limiting the rights of free African Americans? Write five questions that could be answered by historical study, and list resources that you might search for answers to your questions.

DIRECTIONS Read each sentence and fill in the blank with the word in the word pair that best completes the sentence.

1. The ______________________ were the wealthiest members of southern society. (yeomen/planters)
2. Most white southerners were ______________________, or owners of small farms who owned few slaves or none at all. (yeomen/planters)
3. ______________________ would often work side by side with slaves. (Yeomen/Planters)
4. In most southern cities, ______________________ did much of the work. (planters/slaves)
5. White southerners shared a common culture and ______________________ that was central to southern social life. (artisans/religion)
6. Free African Americans in the South often worked as skilled ______________________, or would hire out their services to plantations. (artisans/planters)
7. Some wealthy white southerners attempted to use ______________________ to justify their position in society and the institution of slavery. (artisans/religion)

DIRECTIONS On a separate sheet of paper, use the vocabulary word *yeoman* to write a letter that relates to the lesson.

MAIN IDEAS

1. Slaves faced harsh living conditions in the South.
2. A common African American culture developed in the South, which helped slaves to survive the cruelties of slavery.
3. Slave rebellions drew a harsh response from white southerners.

Key Terms and People

overseers workers hired to watch over and direct the work of slaves

spirituals songs that combine African and European music with religious lyrics

oral tradition passing stories, songs, and poems by word of mouth to preserve heritage and pass down traditions and customs

folktales stories with a moral, often dealing with animal characters and themes of overcoming adversity

Nat Turner Virginia slave who planned to gain freedom by killing slaveholders and their families

Lesson Summary

LIVING UNDER SLAVERY

Agriculture in the South required a lot of workers. Many of those workers were enslaved African Americans. By the mid-1800s slaves accounted for one-third of the population of the South.

Work was the dominant feature of the lives of enslaved people. Men, women, and children were forced to work whenever their slaveholders demanded. Neither sickness nor poor weather was a reason to stop working.

The majority of enslaved people lived and worked on farms or large plantations in the South. Slaves who worked outside were supervised by **overseers**. Other slaves worked indoors, cooking, cleaning, and taking care of the children of the plantation owner.

Not all enslaved people worked on plantations. In cities, some worked as domestic servants,

What did overseers do?

____

____

factory hands, and day laborers. But they still were considered property and had no rights.

Some slaveholders treated their slaves fairly well. Generally this was not out of compassion, but was a way to secure loyal service. Most slaveholders, however, treated their slaves harshly. They used punishments to ensure obedience, including beatings, withholding food, and threatening family members.

What was life like for an enslaved person?

____

____

____

A COMMON CULTURE

A distinctive African American culture emerged in the South. Religion was a cornerstone of the culture. Practicing religion became a way for slaves to resist the power and control of slaveholders. Enslaved African Americans often expressed themselves through **spirituals**. Singing spirituals offered comfort for pain, eased the drudgery of daily work, and bound people together.

Another feature of African American culture was **oral tradition**—the passing down of family histories and heritage by word of mouth. **Folktales**, stories with a moral, were a part of this oral tradition. Many folktales featured a small animal, such as a rabbit, that would defeat a stronger animal, such as a fox, by outwitting it. The stories served to encourage slaves that they could survive the hardships of slavery.

How did slaves keep their culture alive?

____

____

____

Enslaved African Americans found a variety of ways to protest their treatment. Some even ran away. But getting all the way North to freedom was filled with dangers and hardships. Most runaways were caught and forced to return. Some, however, succeeded and escaped to freedom.

Why do you think it was so hard for most runaway slaves to escape to freedom?

____

____

SLAVE REBELLIONS

While it did not happen often, there were violent slave revolts. Some were stopped before they began, and the leaders faced severe punishment, even death. Revolts included the ones planned by Gabriel Prosser in Richmond, Virginia, and Denmark Vesey in Charleston, South Carolina.

The most famous slave revolt was planned by Virginia slave **Nat Turner**. He led a group of slaves as they attacked and killed about 55 white people. In the end, though, more than 100 innocent slaves were killed. When Turner was caught, he said that the revolt was justified and that it was worth dying for. He was executed. As a result of the rebellion, many states strengthened their slave codes.

How did white southerners respond to slave rebellions?

____

____

____

CHALLENGE ACTIVITY

Critical Thinking: Develop Think of challenges that enslaved African Americans faced daily. Write a folktale that would be entertaining and encouraging to a slave. Explain what the characters represent and how the moral applies to life.

folktale	Nat Turner	oral tradition
overseers	spirituals	

DIRECTIONS Answer these questions using terms from the word bank.

1. What is a story with a moral called?

____

____

2. Why was religion part of the culture of African American slaves?

____

____

____

3. Who led the most famous slave revolt in the United States, and what happened to him?

____

____

4. What workers did slaveholders employ to keep slaves under control, and what was their purpose?

____

____

5. How did enslaved African American parents pass their heritage to the next generation?

____

____

Lesson 1

MAIN IDEAS

1. European diseases wiped out much of the Native American population, causing colonists to look for a new labor force.
2. Europeans enslaved millions of Africans and sent them to work in their colonies.
3. Slaves in the Americas created a distinct culture.

Key Terms and People

immune having a natural resistance to a disease

Middle Passage the voyage across the Atlantic that enslaved Africans were forced to endure

African Diaspora the scattering of African people due to slavery

Lesson Summary

THE NEED FOR A NEW LABOR FORCE

Measles, smallpox, and typhus had afflicted Europeans before they came to the New World. As a result, Europeans were more **immune** to the diseases than Native Americans. Native Americans had never been exposed to them. Therefore, these European diseases had a devastating effect on the Native American population. Millions died in the years after Columbus reached the New World.

How did the lack of immunity to disease affect the Native American peoples?

____

____

____

Now the European colonists needed a new workforce for their plantations. Plantations were important to the colonial economic structure. Africans had already developed some immunity to European diseases. The colonists decided that slaves from West Africa could be the solution to the labor problem.

What factors caused colonists to decide to use African slaves?

____

____

____

THE SLAVE TRADE

In 1510 the Spanish government legalized the sale of slaves in its colonies. Over the next century, more than a million African slaves were brought to the Spanish and Portuguese colonies. The English and Dutch were also active slave traders.

Enslaved people were often captured in the interior of Africa. They were chained and forced to march up to 1,000 miles to the coast. They were then chained together and packed as cargo in the lower decks of ships crossing the Atlantic Ocean. This voyage was known as the **Middle Passage**. In the crowded ships, disease spread quickly. Many of the slaves died of sickness, suffocation, or malnutrition during the voyage.

Between the 1520s and the 1860s, about 12 million Africans were shipped across the Atlantic as slaves. The slave trade led to the **African Diaspora**. Slaves had few rights in the colonies and were considered to be property. The treatment of enslaved Africans varied, but severe treatment and dreadful punishments were often part of American slavery.

How many people were shipped from Africa as part of the slave trade?

____

____

SLAVE CULTURE IN THE AMERICAS

Slaves in America came from many parts of Africa. They spoke different languages and had different cultural backgrounds. However, they also shared many customs and viewpoints. They built a new culture on the things they had in common.

Families were a key part of slave culture, but slave families faced many challenges. A family was often broken apart when members were sold to different owners. Religion was a refuge for slaves. Slave religion was primarily Christian, but it also included traditional elements from African religions. Religion gave slaves a sense of self-worth and hope for salvation. Slaves used songs and folktales to tell stories of sorrow, hope, agony, and joy.

Underline the sentence that describes the kind of religion that was common among slaves in the Americas.

CHALLENGE ACTIVITY

Critical Thinking: Elaborate Write a song or folktale that reflects the experiences of enslaved Africans. Your song or folktale should reflect the feelings of sorrow, hope, agony, and joy that were included in the songs and folktales of slaves.

DIRECTIONS Read each sentence and fill in the blank with the word in the word pair that best completes the sentence.

1. Enslaved Africans were forced to endure the ____________________, which took them across the Atlantic Ocean to the Americas. (Middle Passage/plantation agriculture)
2. The slave trade led to the ____________________, or the scattering of enslaved Africans all across the New World. (Middle Passage/African Diaspora)
3. Most adult Europeans were ____________________, or had a natural resistance, to common diseases in Europe like measles, smallpox, and typhus. (enslaved/immune)

DIRECTIONS On the line provided before each statement, write **T** if a statement is true or **F** if a statement is false. If the statement is false, find a word or phrase in the word bank that makes the statement true. Write the new sentence on the line provided.

African Diaspora	immune	Middle Passage

_____ 4. Native Americans had never been exposed to diseases like measles and smallpox, and they were therefore not Middle Passage to them.

____

____

_____ 5. The African Diaspora was the voyage across the Atlantic Ocean in which slaves were chained together and packed as cargo on ships.

____

____

MAIN IDEAS

1. Slaves worked at a variety of jobs on plantations.
2. Life under slavery was difficult and dehumanizing.
3. Slave culture centered around family, community, and religion.
4. Slave uprisings led to stricter slave codes in many states.

Key Terms and People

folktales stories with a moral

spirituals songs that combine African and European music and religious beliefs

Nat Turner Virginia slave who led a rebellion against slaveholders in 1831

Nat Turner's Rebellion the name given to the 1831 rebellion led by Nat Turner

Lesson Summary

SLAVES AND WORK

Most planters used the gang labor system to get their fields farmed. In this system, enslaved men, women, and children over ten years of age all did the same fieldwork from dawn until dark.

Slaves with special skills often were rented out by their owners. Sometimes these slaves were allowed to keep part of what they earned. As a consequence, some skilled slaves were able to save enough money to buy their own freedom.

How could skilled slaves buy their freedom?

____

____

____

LIFE UNDER SLAVERY

To most southern slaveholders, slaves were property, not people. As property, slaves could be bought and sold. Usually, this business occurred at a slave auction. At these auctions, family members could be sold away from each other forever.

Many slaveholders used cruel punishments to make sure their slaves stayed obedient. In addition, many states passed strict slave codes. These laws limited what slaves could do. For example, in some states it was illegal to teach slaves to read and write.

What could happen to family members at a slave auction?

____

____

____

How were laws used to control slaves?

____

____

____

SLAVE CULTURE

For enslaved African Americans, the family was the most important aspect of their lives. Parents made sure their children knew the African part of their history, including African customs and traditions. Since they could not read and write, they passed this information verbally. Some of their stories were **folktales**—stories with morals—to teach children how to survive slavery.

Religion was also an important part of the culture of enslaved African Americans. Christian slaves believed that, in God's eyes, they were equal to anyone else. They held onto the hope that someday they would be freed. Often, these beliefs were expressed in the **spirituals** they sang.

How did slaves keep their culture alive?

____

____

____

SLAVE UPRISINGS

Enslaved African Americans found a variety of ways to protest their treatment. Some even ran away. But getting all the way North to freedom was filled with dangers and hardships. Most runaways were caught and forced to return.

Sometimes, slaves protested with violence. They risked certain punishment. This was true of Virginia slave **Nat Turner**. During **Nat Turner's Rebellion** in 1831, slaves killed about 60 white people. In the end, though, more that 100 slaves were killed and Turner was executed. As a result, many states strengthened their slave codes.

What were the results of Nat Turner's Rebellion?

____

____

____

CHALLENGE ACTIVITY

Critical Thinking: Analyze Write a paragraph explaining why southern slaveholders would want to keep slaves from learning to read and write.

folktale	Nat Turner's Rebellion	slave codes
Nat Turner	spirituals	

DIRECTIONS Answer each question by writing a sentence that contains at least one word from the word bank.

1. What was a story with a moral called?

____

____

2. What did some slaves use to express their religious beliefs?

____

____

3. Who led the most violent slave revolt in the United States?

____

____

4. What event in 1831 led to the death of about 60 white people in Virginia?

____

____

5. What was one way slaveholders attempted to keep slaves under control?

____

____

Name ______________________ Class ______________ Date __________

Slavery in the United States

Lesson 3

MAIN IDEAS

1. Americans from a variety of backgrounds actively opposed slavery.
2. Abolitionists organized the Underground Railroad to help enslaved Africans escape.
3. Despite efforts of abolitionists, many Americans remained opposed to ending slavery.

Key Terms and People

abolition complete end to slavery

Elihu Embree Quaker who opposed slavery and published *The Emancipator*

William Lloyd Garrison abolitionist who ran the *Liberator* newspaper and also helped found the American Anti-Slavery Society

American Anti-Slavery Society organization that wanted immediate emancipation and racial equality

Angelina and Sarah Grimké southern sisters who spoke in favor of abolition

Frederick Douglass ex-slave who became a pro-abolition speaker

Sojourner Truth ex-slave who spoke for abolition and women's rights

Underground Railroad loosely organized group that helped slaves escape from the South

Harriet Tubman ex-slave who freed more than 300 others using the Underground Railroad

Lesson Summary

AMERICANS OPPOSE SLAVERY

Some Americans had opposed slavery even before the country was founded. Benjamin Franklin was the president of the first antislavery society in America.

DIFFERENCES AMONG ABOLITIONISTS

By the 1830s, many Americans formed a movement to abolish, or end, slavery. They supported **abolition**. These abolitionists worked for emancipation, or freedom from slavery, for all who lived in the United States.

What is the difference between abolition and emancipation?

____

____

____

The Quakers were among the first people to oppose slavery. They did so on religious grounds. **Elihu Embree** published the first newspaper devoted to abolition. It was called *The Emancipator*.

Many abolitionists spread the message of abolition using the power of the pen. **William Lloyd Garrison**, for example, ran the *Liberator* newspaper. He also helped found the **American Anti-Slavery Society**. This group believed in emancipation and racial equality. **Angelina and Sarah Grimké** were two sisters from a southern slaveholding family. They wrote pamphlets and a book to try to convince other white people to join the fight against slavery.

Name two newspapers published for the cause of abolition.

____

____

When **Frederick Douglass** was a slave, he secretly learned to read and write. After he escaped slavery, he used those skills to support the abolition movement. He published a newspaper called the *North Star*. He also wrote books about his life as a slave. Douglass was a powerful speaker who vividly described slavery's horrors. Many other ex-slaves also were active abolitionists. One example was **Sojourner Truth**, who gave dramatic antislavery speeches.

Why do you think Frederick Douglass had to learn to read and write in secret?

____

____

____

THE UNDERGROUND RAILROAD

The **Underground Railroad** was the name given to a loosely knit group of white and black abolitionists who helped escaped slaves get North to freedom. One of the most famous "conductors" on this Railroad was an ex-slave named **Harriet Tubman**. She made 19 trips to the North, freeing more than 300 slaves.

What do you think would happen to someone who was caught helping slaves escape?

____

____

____

OPPOSITION TO ENDING SLAVERY

Many white southerners felt slavery was vital to their economy. They also felt that outsiders should not tell them what to do. Some justified enslaving people by claiming that African

Americans needed the structure of slavery to survive.

CHALLENGE ACTIVITY

Critical Thinking: Make Inferences Why do you think Frederick Douglass called his newspaper the *North Star*?

DIRECTIONS Write two adjectives or descriptive phrases that describe the term.

1. abolition ____

____

2. American Anti-Slavery Society ____________________________

____

3. Elihu Embree ____

____

4. Angelina and Sarah Grimké _______________________________

____

5. Frederick Douglass ______________________________________

____

6. Harriet Tubman ____

____

7. the *Liberator* ____

____

8. Underground Railroad ____________________________________

____

9. William Lloyd Garrison ___________________________________

____

DIRECTIONS On the line provided before each statement, write **T** if a statement is true and **F** if a statement is false. If the statement is false, write the correct term on the line after each sentence that makes the sentence a true statement.

______10. Some people who opposed slavery on religious grounds began working for the Underground Railroad.

____

______11. Harriet Tubman gave dramatic antislavery speeches.

____

______12. William Lloyd Garrison published an abolitionist newspaper called the *Liberator* and helped found the American Anti-Slavery Society.

____

______13. The most famous conductor on the Underground Railroad was Frederick Douglass.

____

Name ______________________ Class ______________ Date __________

Lesson 4

MAIN IDEAS

1. The addition of new land in the West renewed disputes over the expansion of slavery.
2. The Compromise of 1850 tried to solve the disputes over slavery.
3. The Fugitive Slave Act caused more controversy and led to the growth of antislavery leanings.

Key Terms and People

Wilmot Proviso suggested bill that would outlaw slavery in new U.S. territory

sectionalism situation in which people favor the interests of one region over those of the entire country

Free-Soil Party third political party that formed to support abolition

Compromise of 1850 law that maintained America's slave-state/free-state balance

secede formally withdraw

Fugitive Slave Act law that made it a crime to aid runaway slaves

Anthony Burns Virginia fugitive slave whose attempted rescue from a Boston jail ended in violence

Uncle Tom's Cabin antislavery novel written by Harriet Beecher Stowe

Harriet Beecher Stowe author of the antislavery novel, *Uncle Tom's Cabin*

Lesson Summary

SLAVERY AND TERRITORIAL EXPANSION

The nation's debate over slavery continued as the country got bigger. Many northerners, for example, supported the **Wilmot Proviso**, which would outlaw slavery in new lands. Many southerners, on the other hand, did not support the bill.

Arguments about the proviso showed how **sectionalism** was dividing the country. Because the two major political parties could not agree on slavery, a third party, the **Free-Soil Party**, formed to support abolition.

Why do you think southerners were opposed to the Wilmot Proviso?

____

____

____

ANOTHER ATTEMPT AT COMPROMISE

The **Compromise of 1850** was presented by Kentucky's Henry Clay. Its purpose was to maintain the delicate balance between slave and free states. The compromise was necessary in part because some southerners thought their states should **secede** from the Union.

What made Henry Clay's law a compromise?

____

____

____

THE CRISIS DEEPENS

Part of the Compromise of 1850 required passage of the **Fugitive Slave Act**. This act made it a crime to help runaway slaves. Abolitionists especially reacted in anger to the compromise. Sometimes that anger turned to violence. This was true when abolitionists tried to rescue Virginia fugitive **Anthony Burns** from a Boston jail.

How can you tell that Anthony Burns was a slave?

____

____

____

Many abolitionists expressed their antislavery feelings in speeches. Others used the written word to influence people on the issue of slavery. One effective author was **Harriet Beecher Stowe**. In 1852 Stowe's antislavery novel, ***Uncle Tom's Cabin***, was published. The book showed some of the consequences of slavery. It sold more than 2 million copies and influenced many to support the end of slavery.

How did Harriet Beecher Stowe impact the issue of slavery in America?

____

____

____

CHALLENGE ACTIVITY

Critical Thinking: Make Generalizations Write a paragraph about something you read or saw that made you change your mind. It could be a book, a speech, a television show—even a teacher.

DIRECTIONS Read each sentence and fill in the blank with the word in the word pair that best completes the sentence.

1. The ________________________ was a suggested bill that would outlaw slavery in new U.S. territory. (Fugitive Slave Act/Wilmot Proviso)
2. When people favor the interests of one region over those of the entire country, this is called ________________________. (Compromise of 1850/ sectionalism)
3. Before the Compromise of 1850, some southerners thought their states might ________________________ from the Union. (take slaves/secede)
4. ________________________ was the author of an antislavery novel called ________________________. (Anthony Burns/Harriet Beecher Stowe); (Compromise of 1850/*Uncle Tom's Cabin*)
5. ________________________, a Virginia fugitive, was arrested in Boston and eventually returned to slavery in Virginia. (Anthony Burns/Daniel Webster)
6. Antislavery northerners formed a third party called the ________________________. (Free-Soil Party/Wilmot Proviso)
7. The purpose of the ________________________ was to maintain the balance between slave and free states. (Compromise of 1850/Wilmot Proviso)
8. The ________________________ made it a crime to help runaway slaves. (Fugitive Slave Act/Wilmot Proviso)

Name ______________________ Class ______________ Date __________

Reform Movements in the United States

Lesson 1

MAIN IDEAS

1. Millions of immigrants, mostly German and Irish, arrived in the United States despite anti-immigrant movements.
2. Industrialization led to the growth of cities.
3. American cities experienced urban problems due to rapid growth.

Key Terms and People

nativists people who opposed immigration

Know-Nothing Party political organization founded by nativists in 1849

middle class a social and economic level between the wealthy and the poor

tenements dirty, unsafe housing structures in which the cities' poor were forced to live

Lesson Summary

MILLIONS OF IMMIGRANTS ARRIVE

Between 1840 and 1860, more than 4 million immigrants came to the United States. Many came from Ireland, fleeing starvation that came from the potato blight there. Many Irish immigrants arrived poor. These immigrants often got jobs working long hours for little pay.

Compare and contrast Irish and German immigrants between 1840 and 1860.

____

____

____

Unlike the Irish, immigrants from Germany often arrived with some money. Many came to America after a revolution in their homeland. Others came for the opportunities America offered. Many bought farmland in America's Midwest. Others settled and worked in cities.

To many native-born Americans, the new immigrants posed a threat. Americans worried that immigrants would take away their jobs. Immigrants would do the same work but for less money. The Americans also mistrusted Catholic immigrants. In Europe, Protestants and Catholics had a history of conflicts.

Americans who opposed immigration for these reasons were known as **nativists**. Together, the nativists formed a political group called the **Know-Nothing Party**, which tried to limit immigration.

Why did nativists worry about the increasing numbers of immigrants?

____

____

____

RAPID GROWTH OF CITIES

In the mid-1800s, the Industrial Revolution encouraged rapid growth in America's cities. The jobs the Industrial Revolution created also helped build a **middle class**—a social and economic level between the wealthy and the poor. People enjoyed the culture in America's cities. Libraries, clubs, and theaters grew as the cities grew.

Why do you think culture changed after the Industrial Revolution?

____

____

____

URBAN PROBLEMS

Many people, especially immigrants, who moved to the city to work could afford only tenement rents. **Tenements** were poorly designed apartment buildings that were dirty, overcrowded, and unsafe. Cities had not yet learned how to deal with the filth and garbage generated by so many people, and epidemics were common. Crime and fires also plagued the fast-growing cities of the United States.

Why were living conditions so poor in urban areas?

____

____

____

CHALLENGE ACTIVITY

Critical Thinking: Summarize List some of the health and safety issues that plagued America's cities during the first half of the 1800s.

immigrants	Know-Nothing Party	middle class
nativists	tenements	

DIRECTIONS Read each sentence and choose the correct term from the word bank to replace the underlined phrase. Write the term in the space provided and then define the term in your own words.

1. A new social class, the nativists, occupied a social and economic level between the wealthy and the poor. ______________________

   Your definition: ______________________

   ____

2. Many city dwellers could only afford to live in poorly designed housing structures called immigrants. ______________________

   Your definition: ______________________

   ____

3. The nativists founded a political organization called the middle class.

   ____

   Your definition: ______________________

   ____

4. Tenements were Americans who held views such as fearing that new immigrants might work for lower wages and take away their jobs.

   ____

   Your definition: ______________________

   ____

5. In the mid-1800s, a flood of nativists crossed the Atlantic Ocean to begin new lives in the United States. ______________________

   Your definition: ______________________

   ____

Lesson 2

MAIN IDEAS

1. Transcendentalists and utopian communities withdrew from American society.
2. American Romantic painters and writers made important contributions to art and literature.

Key Terms and People

transcendentalism belief that people should rise above material things in life and that people should depend on themselves rather than outside authority

Ralph Waldo Emerson American writer most famous for his essay "Self-Reliance"

Margaret Fuller American writer who wrote and edited material on transcendentalism

Henry David Thoreau American writer most famous for the transcendental ideas he summarized in his book *Walden*

utopian communities experimental communities that tried to create a perfect society

Nathaniel Hawthorne American writer best known for his novel *The Scarlet Letter*

Edgar Allan Poe American writer best known for his short stories and poetry

Emily Dickinson American poet whose poems were published after her death

Henry Wadsworth Longfellow American poet who wrote popular story-poems like *The Song of Hiawatha*

Walt Whitman American poet best known for his poetry collection *Leaves of Grass*

Lesson Summary

TRANSCENDENTALISTS

Transcendentalism was a belief system in which followers thought they could rise above the material things in life. Transcendentalists believed that people should depend on themselves. **Ralph Waldo Emerson**, **Margaret Fuller**, and **Henry David Thoreau** were transcendentalists.

Name two transcendentalist thinkers.

____

____

Emerson expressed his ideas in the essay "Self-Reliance." Fuller edited a publication called *The Dial*. Thoreau advised simple living. He wrote his book *Walden* after he lived at Walden Pond for two years.

Some transcendentalists created communities away from society. In these **utopian communities**, people hoped to form a perfect society. People in utopian communities pursued abstract spirituality and cooperative lifestyles.

Why might transcendentalists seek to create utopian communities?

____

____

____

AMERICAN ROMANTICISM

In the early and mid-1800s, many artists were inspired by simple life and nature's beauty.

At this time American Romantic writers began to develop an American style. Ann Sophia Stephens wrote popular historical fiction. *The Scarlet Letter* by **Nathaniel Hawthorne** described Puritan life in America. Herman Melville wrote *Moby Dick*, considered one of America's finest novels. **Edgar Allan Poe** also gained fame for his short stories and poetry. "The Raven" is the most well known of his poems.

Emily Dickinson and **Henry Wadsworth Longfellow** are two poets of this time. **Walt Whitman** wrote the poetry book *Leaves of Grass*, which praises American individualism and democracy.

Underline all the writers' names that appear in this section. Put an X by the names you have heard before.

Circle the titles of famous novels written by American Romantics.

CHALLENGE ACTIVITY

Critical Thinking: Make Inferences In this section certain writers' names appear in bold print, while other names do not. Explain what you think the difference is and why it is important.

DIRECTIONS Write two adjectives or descriptive phrases that describe the term or person.

1. Edgar Allan Poe ____
____
2. Emily Dickinson____
____
3. Henry David Thoreau ____
____
4. Nathaniel Hawthorne ____
____
5. Ralph Waldo Emerson _______________________________________
____
6. Henry Wadsworth Longfellow __________________________________
____
7. transcendentalism ____
____
8. utopian communities _______________________________________
____
9. Walt Whitman ____
____

DIRECTIONS Read each sentence and fill in the blank with the word in the word pair that best completes the sentence.

10. "The Raven" is the most famous work by writer and poet _______________________. (Ralph Waldo Emerson/Edgar Allan Poe)
11. _______________________ wrote *Leaves of Grass*. (Nathaniel Hawthorne/ Walt Whitman)
12. _______________________ edited the transcendentalist publication *The Dial*. (Margaret Fuller/Emily Dickenson)
13. One of the best-known pieces of Romantic literature is *The Scarlet Letter*, a novel by New England writer ____________________. (Nathaniel Hawthorne/Walt Whitman)

Name ______________________ Class ______________________ Date ____________

Lesson 3

MAIN IDEAS

1. The Second Great Awakening sparked interest in religion.
2. Social reformers began to speak out about temperance and prison reform.
3. Improvements in education reform affected many segments of the population.
4. Northern African American communities became involved in reform efforts.

Key Terms and People

Second Great Awakening late 1700s–early 1800s movement of Christian renewal

Charles Grandison Finney minister who challenged some traditional beliefs

Lyman Beecher minister who spoke against both Charles Grandison Finney and alcohol consumption

temperance movement movement to encourage people not to drink alcohol

Dorothea Dix prison reformer

common-school movement movement to have all children, regardless of background, taught in a common place

Horace Mann education reformer

Catharine Beecher founder of all-female academy in Hartford, Connecticut

Thomas Gallaudet education reformer for the hearing impaired

Lesson Summary

SECOND GREAT AWAKENING

During the 1790s and early 1800s, a period of Christian renewal began. It was known as the **Second Great Awakening**. By the 1830s, it had swept through parts of New York and the frontier.

Charles Grandison Finney was one of the leaders of the Second Great Awakening. Some did not agree with Finney's message, including Boston minister **Lyman Beecher**. However, the Constitution's First Amendment guaranteed Finney's right to speak and be heard. Through the efforts of Finney and other ministers, many Americans joined churches across the country.

What can you infer from the fact that this period was called the Second Great Awakening?

____

____

____

SOCIAL REFORMERS SPEAK OUT

In the spirit of the Second Great Awakening, people tried to reform many of society's ills. In the **temperance movement**, people tried to limit alcohol consumption. Lyman Beecher and other ministers spoke about the evils of alcohol.

Dorothea Dix reported on the terrible conditions she found when she visited some Massachusetts prisons. Imprisoned along with adult criminals were the mentally ill and children. Because of efforts by Dix and others, governments built hospitals for the mentally ill and reform schools for young lawbreakers. They also began to try to reform—not just punish—prisoners.

How did prisons change as a result of reformers like Dorothea Dix?

____

____

____

IMPROVEMENTS IN EDUCATION

Education in the early 1800s improved with the **common-school movement**. This movement, led by **Horace Mann**, worked to have all students, regardless of background, taught in the same place. Women's education also improved at this time. Several women's schools, including **Catharine Beecher's** all-female academy in Connecticut, opened. Teaching people with disabilities improved, too. For example, **Thomas Gallaudet** bettered the education of the hearing impaired.

What was the common-school movement?

____

____

____

Circle the names of all the reformers on this page who worked to better America during this time.

AFRICAN AMERICAN COMMUNITIES

In this period, life improved for the nation's free black population. The Free African Religious Society, founded by Richard Allen, pressed for equality and education. Leaders such as Alexander Crummel helped build African American schools in New York, Philadelphia, and other cities. In 1835 Oberlin College became the first college to admit African Americans. Soon after, in the 1840s, several African American colleges were founded.

CHALLENGE ACTIVITY

Critical Thinking: Compare What did Horace Mann, Catharine Beecher, Thomas Gallaudet, Richard Allen, and Alexander Crummel all have in common?

Catharine Beecher	Lyman Beecher	common-school movement
Dorothea Dix	Charles Grandison Finney	Thomas Gallaudet
Horace Mann	Second Great Awakening	temperance movement

DIRECTIONS On the line provided before each statement, write **T** if a statement is true and **F** if a statement is false. If the statement is false, write the correct term on the line after each sentence that makes the sentence a true statement.

_____ 1. Thomas Gallaudet bettered the education and lives of people with hearing impairments.

____

_____ 2. An all-female academy in Connecticut was started by Dorothea Dix.

____

_____ 3. Lyman Beecher was a leader of the common-school movement.

____

_____ 4. People in the common-school movement wanted all children taught in a common place, regardless of background.

____

_____ 5. Catharine Beecher was a middle-class reformer who helped change the American prison system.

____

_____ 6. Minister Horace Mann spoke widely about the evils of alcohol.

____

_____ 7. A social reform effort that urged people to use self-discipline to stop drinking hard liquor was called the temperance movement.

____

_____ 8. Charles Grandison Finney was one of the most important leaders of the Second Great Awakening.

____

Name ______________________________ Class ____________________ Date ____________

MAIN IDEAS

1. Abolitionist leaders used a variety of methods in their campaign against slavery in the United States.
2. The Underground Railroad was an informal network that helped enslaved Africans escape to freedom.
3. Even as the movement grew, many Americans remained opposed to ending slavery.

Key Terms and People

abolition movement campaign to end slavery

William Lloyd Garrison abolitionist who ran the *Liberator* newspaper and also helped found the American Anti-Slavery Society

American Anti-Slavery Society organization that wanted immediate emancipation and racial equality

Lucretia Mott founder of Philadelphia Female Anti-Slavery Society

Angelina and Sarah Grimké southern sisters who spoke in favor of abolition

Frederick Douglass ex-slave who became a pro-abolition speaker

Sojourner Truth ex-slave who spoke for abolition and women's rights

Underground Railroad loosely organized network of people that helped slaves escape from the South

Harriet Tubman escaped slave who freed more than 300 others using the Underground Railroad

Lesson Summary

DEMANDING AN END TO SLAVERY

The **abolition movement** was a movement to end slavery. The movement grew into one of the largest reform movements of the mid-1800s. Supporters of abolition were called abolitionists. Men and women, blacks and whites, from both the North and the South were abolitionists.

The rebirth of religious feelings in the Second Great Awakening contributed to a larger number of people opposed to slavery. Many religious people saw slavery as a moral wrong.

How did the Second Great Awakening contribute to the abolition movement?

____

____

Antislavery reformers did not always agree with each other. Some believed that African Americans should be treated as equal to white Americans. Others thought there should be some political and social differences.

Over what ideas did antislavery reformers disagree?

____

Many abolitionists contributed to the movement. **William Lloyd Garrison**, for example, ran the *Liberator* newspaper. He also helped found the **American Anti-Slavery Society**. This group called for the immediate end to slavery in the United States. **Lucretia Mott** founded the Philadelphia Female Anti-Slavery Society in 1833 because women were not allowed to join the American Anti-Slavery Society. **Angelina and Sarah Grimké** were two sisters from a southern slaveholding family. The book they wrote, *American Slavery As It Is*, was one of the most important antislavery works of its time.

Why were there two Anti-Slavery Societies?

____

Because **Frederick Douglass** had been a slave, he spoke from experience. His writings and powerful speeches convinced some people slavery was wrong. Many other ex-slaves also were active abolitionists. One was **Sojourner Truth**, who became famous for her antislavery speeches.

ESCAPE TO THE NORTH

The **Underground Railroad** was not an actual railroad. It was the name given to a network of white and black abolitionists who helped escaped slaves travel to free territory. One of the most famous "conductors" on this Railroad was an escaped slave named **Harriet Tubman**. She made nearly 20 trips to the North, freeing more than 300 slaves.

What did the Underground Railroad do?

____

OPPOSING ABOLITION

Many white southerners felt slavery was vital to their economy. They also felt that outsiders should not tell them what to do. Some

Why did some people oppose abolition?

____

northerners feared that freed slaves would take jobs away from white people.

CHALLENGE ACTIVITY

Critical Thinking: Make Inferences Why do you think people would want to hear speeches by Frederick Douglass and Sojourner Truth?

DIRECTIONS Write two adjectives or descriptive phrases that describe the term.

1. abolition movement ______________________________

2. American Anti-Slavery Society ______________________________

3. Philadelphia Female Anti-Slavery Society ______________________________

4. Angelina and Sarah Grimké ______________________________

5. Frederick Douglass ______________________________

6. Harriet Tubman ______________________________

7. the *Liberator* ______________________________

8. Underground Railroad ______________________________

9. William Lloyd Garrison ______________________________

DIRECTIONS On the line provided before each statement, write T if a statement is true and F is a statement is false. If the statement is false, write the correct term on the line after each sentence that makes the sentence a true statement.

_____10. Some people who opposed slavery on religious grounds began working for the Underground Railroad.

____

_____11. Frederick Douglass wrote one of the most important antislavery works of its time, *American Slavery As It Is*.

____

_____12. William Lloyd Garrison published an abolitionist newspaper called the *Liberator* and helped found the American Anti-Slavery Society.

____

_____13. The most famous conductor on the Underground Railroad was Lucretia Mott.

____

Name ______________________________ Class ____________________ Date ____________

MAIN IDEAS

1. Influenced by the abolition movement, many women struggled to gain equal rights for themselves.
2. Calls for women's rights met opposition from men and women.
3. The Seneca Falls Convention launched the first organized women's rights movement in the United States.

Key Terms and People

Elizabeth Cady Stanton supporter of women's rights who helped organize the Seneca Falls Convention; co-founder of Woman Suffrage Association

Seneca Falls Convention the first organized public meeting about women's rights held in the United States

Declaration of Sentiments document officially requesting equal rights for women

Lucy Stone spokesperson for the Anti-Slavery Society and the women's rights movement; co-founder of Woman Suffrage Association

Susan B. Anthony women's rights supporter who argued for equal pay for equal work, the right of women to enter male professions, and property rights

Matilda Joslyn Gage co-founder of National Woman Suffrage Association; writer and advocate for women's rights

Lesson Summary

WOMEN'S STRUGGLE FOR EQUAL RIGHTS

In the mid-1800s, some female abolitionists also began to focus on the women's rights in America, despite their many critics. For example, the Grimké sisters were criticized for speaking in public. Their critics felt they should stay at home. Sarah Grimké responded by writing a pamphlet in support of women's rights. She also argued for equal educational opportunities and laws that treated women in an equal manner.

Abolitionist Sojourner Truth also became a women's rights supporter. The ex-slave never learned to read or write, but she became a great and influential speaker.

Why did critics of the Grimké sisters think women should not speak in public?

____

____

OPPOSING THE CALL FOR WOMEN'S RIGHTS

The women's movement had many critics—both men and women. Some felt a woman should stay home. Others felt women were not as physically or mentally strong as men. Therefore, they needed the protection of first their fathers, then their husbands. This was why upon marriage husbands took control of their wives' property.

What arguments did critics use against women's rights?

____

____

____

SENECA FALLS CONVENTION

Elizabeth Cady Stanton and Lucretia Mott organized the **Seneca Falls Convention**. It opened July 19, 1848, in Seneca Falls, New York. The convention was the first public meeting about women's rights in the United States. It resulted in the **Declaration of Sentiments**. This document officially requested equality for women. It brought 18 charges against men, much as the Declaration of Independence had brought 18 charges against King George III.

Why was the Seneca Falls Convention important?

____

____

____

After the convention, more women rose to lead the fight for rights. **Lucy Stone** was a gifted speaker for the Anti-Slavery Society. She used her speaking skills to persuade others to support the rights of women. **Susan B. Anthony** argued that women should be paid the same as men for the same job, and that women could do the jobs reserved for men. **Matilda Joslyn Gage** published *National Citizen and Ballot Box*, a newspaper promoting women's right to vote.

Why do you think most of the leaders in the women's rights movement were women?

____

____

____

CHALLENGE ACTIVITY

Critical Thinking: Evaluate Identify the women you think had the greatest impact on women's rights. Write a sentence or two explaining your choice.

DIRECTIONS Read each sentence and fill in the blank with the word in the word pair that best completes the sentence.

1. ______________________ wrote about women's rights issues and published *National Citizen and Ballot Box*. (Matilda Joslyn Gage/Elizabeth Cady Stanton)
2. A well-known spokesperson for the Anti-Slavery Society who took up the cause of women's rights was ____________________. (Lucy Stone/Susan B. Anthony)
3. A powerful speaker for both abolition and women's rights was ______________________, who had been born into slavery. (Sojourner Truth/Lucy Stone)
4. The ______________________ was the first public meeting to discuss women's rights. (Seneca Falls Convention/Declaration of Sentiments)
5. Convention organizers wrote a document called the ______________________ that detailed their beliefs about social injustice toward women. (Seneca Falls Convention/Declaration of Sentiments)
6. ______________________ argued that women should have jobs equal to men and be paid the same wage. (Elizabeth Cady Stanton/Susan B. Anthony)
7. ______________________ wrote a pamphlet in support of women's rights. (Sojourner Truth/Sarah Grimké)

Name ______________________ Class ______________ Date __________

A Divided Nation

Lesson 1

MAIN IDEAS

1. The addition of new land in the West renewed disputes over the expansion of slavery.
2. The Compromise of 1850 tried to solve the disputes over slavery.
3. The Fugitive Slave Act caused more controversy.
4. Abolitionists used antislavery literature to promote opposition.

Key Terms and People

Wilmot Proviso suggested bill that would outlaw slavery in new U.S. territory

sectionalism situation in which people favor the interests of one region over those of the entire country

popular sovereignty the idea that political power belongs to the people

Free-Soil Party third political party that formed to support abolition

secede formally withdraw

Compromise of 1850 law that maintained America's slave-state/free-state balance

Fugitive Slave Act law that made it a crime to aid runaway slaves

Anthony Burns fugitive slave from Virginia whose attempted rescue from a Boston jail ended in violence

Harriet Beecher Stowe author of the antislavery novel *Uncle Tom's Cabin*

Uncle Tom's Cabin antislavery novel written by Harriet Beecher Stowe

Lesson Summary

NEW LAND RENEWS SLAVERY DISPUTES

The nation's debate over slavery continued as the country got bigger. Many northerners supported the **Wilmot Proviso**. That bill would outlaw slavery in new parts of the country. Many southerners did not support the bill. Arguments about the Wilmot Proviso demonstrated how **sectionalism** was dividing the country.

Why do you think southerners were opposed to the Wilmot Proviso?

____

____

____

Some favored the idea of **popular sovereignty**. They thought each region's voters should decide the question of slavery for that region. The debate was so intense that a third political party, the **Free-Soil Party**, formed to support abolition.

COMPROMISE OF 1850

Henry Clay had a plan to keep the balance between slave and free states. John C. Calhoun thought the plan would lead to a civil war. He asked that slave states be allowed to **secede**. To solve the dispute, both sides gave up something and created the **Compromise of 1850**. California would be a free state. The issue of slavery would be decided by popular sovereignty in Utah and New Mexico.

What made Henry Clay's plan a compromise?

____

____

____

FUGITIVE SLAVE ACT

Part of the Compromise of 1850 required passage of the **Fugitive Slave Act**. This act made it a crime to help runaway slaves. Abolitionists reacted in anger to the compromise. Sometimes that anger turned to violence. This was true when abolitionists tried to rescue Virginia fugitive **Anthony Burns** from a Boston jail.

How can you tell that Anthony Burns was a slave?

____

____

____

ANTISLAVERY LITERATURE

Many abolitionists expressed their antislavery feelings in speeches. Others used the written word to influence people on the issue of slavery. One effective author was **Harriet Beecher Stowe**. Stowe's antislavery novel, ***Uncle Tom's Cabin***, was published in 1852. The book showed some of the consequences of slavery. It sold more than 2 million copies and influenced many to support the end of slavery.

How did Harriet Beecher Stowe impact the issue of slavery in America?

____

____

____

CHALLENGE ACTIVITY

Critical Thinking: Explain Write a paragraph about a time when you had to give up something to get something else you wanted. Explain how your compromise worked.

DIRECTIONS Read each sentence and fill in the blank with the word in the word pair that best completes the sentence.

1. The _______________________ proposed that slavery be outlawed in new parts of the country. (Fugitive Slave Act/Wilmot Proviso)
2. When people favor the interests of one region over those of the entire country, this is called _______________________. (popular sovereignty/ sectionalism)
3. _______________________ would occur if voters in a new territory were able to decide if they wanted to ban or allow slavery. (Popular sovereignty/ Sectionalism)
4. _______________________ was the author of an antislavery novel called _______________________. (Anthony Burns/Harriet Beecher Stowe); (Compromise of 1850/*Uncle Tom's Cabin*)
5. _______________________, a Virginia fugitive, was arrested in Boston and eventually returned to slavery in Virginia. (Anthony Burns/Daniel Webster)
6. Antislavery northerners formed a third party called the _______________________. (Free-Soil Party/Wilmot Proviso)
7. A plan by _______________________ led to the _______________________, which allowed California to enter the Union as a free state, while the question of slavery in Utah and New Mexico would be decided by popular sovereignty. (Anthony Burns/Henry Clay); (Compromise of 1850/Wilmot Proviso)
8. _______________________ of South Carolina was against the Compromise of 1850 and thought slave states should be allowed to secede. (John C. Calhoun/Harriet Beecher Stowe)
9. The _______________________ made it a crime to help runaway slaves. (Fugitive Slave Act/Wilmot Proviso)

Name ______________________ Class ______________ Date __________

A Divided Nation

Lesson 2

MAIN IDEAS

1. The debate over the expansion of slavery influenced the election of 1852.
2. The Kansas-Nebraska Act allowed voters to allow or prohibit slavery.
3. Pro-slavery and antislavery groups clashed violently in what became known as "Bleeding Kansas."

Key Terms and People

Franklin Pierce Democratic candidate who won the presidential election of 1852

Stephen Douglas senator who introduced what would become the Kansas-Nebraska Act

Kansas-Nebraska Act the law that divided the rest of the Louisiana Purchase into two territories—Kansas and Nebraska

Pottawatomie Massacre the murder of five pro-slavery men at Pottawatomie Creek by John Brown and several other abolitionists

Preston Brooks South Carolina representative who used a cane to beat Charles Sumner on the Senate floor for his criticisms of pro-slavery leaders

Charles Sumner Massachusetts senator who was an outspoken critic of pro-slavery leaders

Lesson Summary

ELECTION OF 1852

In the presidential election of 1852, the Democrats nominated **Franklin Pierce**. He was not a well-known politician, but his promise to honor the Compromise of 1850 assured him many southern votes. Pierce ran against Whig candidate Winfield Scott. He was a candidate Southerners did not trust because he had failed to support the Compromise of 1850. Pierce won the election by a huge margin.

Why was Franklin Pierce a popular candidate in the South?

____

____

THE KANSAS-NEBRASKA ACT

The slavery issue continued to plague the country. In 1854 **Stephen Douglas** introduced the **Kansas-Nebraska Act**, which addressed slavery in the

Louisiana Territory. It got its name from the two territories into which it divided the rest of Louisiana—Kansas and Nebraska. In each territory, popular sovereignty would determine the slavery question. The act ended the restriction placed on slavery by the Missouri Compromise. Northern abolitionists were upset about the act's implications.

How did the Kansas-Nebraska Act get its name?

____

____

To make sure Kansas voted in favor of slavery, pro-slavery voters left their homes in Missouri. They crossed the border to vote in Kansas. They won and quickly set up a pro-slavery government. However, those who did not believe in slavery set up a separate government in Topeka.

What do you think would be the consequences of one state having two governments?

____

____

____

"BLEEDING KANSAS"

In May 1856 pro-slavery jurors charged antislavery leaders with treason. Pro-slavery forces rode to Lawrence to arrest those charged. When they found the suspects had fled, they burned and looted the town.

What caused the Sack of Lawrence?

____

____

The Sack of Lawrence outraged many abolitionists, including John Brown of New England. Together with a group, Brown was responsible for the **Pottawatomie Massacre**, in which five pro-slavery men were killed. Quickly, Kansas fell into civil war.

Fighting even took place on the Senate floor. South Carolina representative **Preston Brooks** used his cane to beat Massachusetts senator **Charles Sumner** into unconsciousness because of Sumner's criticisms of pro-slavery leaders.

Was Senator Charles Sumner for or against slavery?

____

CHALLENGE ACTIVITY

Critical Thinking: Explain Write a few sentences to explain how Kansas got the nickname "Bleeding Kansas."

Charles Sumner	Kansas-Nebraska Act	Preston Brooks
Franklin Pierce	Pottawatomie Massacre	Stephen Douglas
John Brown		

DIRECTIONS On the line provided before each statement, write **T** if a statement is true and **F** if a statement is false. If the statement is false, write the correct term on the line after each sentence that makes the sentence a true statement.

______ 1. Franklin Pierce attacked Charles Sumner in the Senate chamber and beat him unconscious with a cane.

____

______ 2. Democratic candidate Stephen Douglas won the presidential election of 1852.

____

______ 3. Preston Brooks, a senator from Massachusetts, spoke out against the pro-slavery people in Kansas and was beaten by a fellow senator.

____

______ 4. The Pottawatomie Massacre resulted in the deaths of five pro-slavery men in Kansas.

____

______ 5. Senator Stephen Douglas introduced the Kansas-Nebraska Act.

____

______ 6. The Kansas-Nebraska Act divided part of the Louisiana Purchase into two territories—Kansas and Nebraska.

____

______ 7. In 1855 abolitionist John Brown and his sons were responsible for the massacre of five pro-slavery men that led to a civil war in Kansas.

____

______ 8. The Pottawatomie Massacre removed the Missouri Compromise's restriction on slavery.

____

MAIN IDEAS

1. Political parties in the United States underwent change due to the movement to expand slavery.
2. The *Dred Scott* decision created further division over the issue of slavery.
3. The Lincoln-Douglas debates brought much attention to the conflict over slavery.

Key Terms and People

Republican Party political party founded to fight slavery and its spread to the West

James Buchanan Democratic candidate and winner of the 1856 presidential election

John C. Frémont Republican candidate for the 1856 presidential election; against spread of slavery

Dred Scott slave who unsuccessfully sued for his freedom in 1846

Roger B. Taney Chief Justice of the Supreme Court during the *Dred Scott* decision

Abraham Lincoln early leader of the Republican Party

Lincoln-Douglas debates debates between senatorial candidates Abraham Lincoln and Stephen Douglas

Freeport Doctrine Stephen Douglas's belief that popular sovereignty made the decisions of citizens more important than decisions made by the Supreme Court in the *Dred Scott* case

Lesson Summary

POLITICAL PARTIES UNDERGO CHANGE

As the 1850s progressed, Whigs, Democrats, Free-Soilers, and abolitionists united. They formed the **Republican Party** to fight slavery. Others left their parties to form the Know-Nothing Party. For the 1856 presidential election, the old Democratic Party nominated **James Buchanan**. Buchanan had been out of the country during the "Bleeding Kansas" dispute. He defeated Know-Nothing Millard Fillmore and Republican **John C. Frémont**.

Why might it matter to voters that James Buchanan had been out of the country during "Bleeding Kansas"?

____

____

____

DRED SCOTT DECISION

Dred Scott was a slave. His slaveowner was a doctor who traveled from Missouri, a slave state, to free areas and back again to Missouri. Scott sued for his freedom, since he had lived in free areas.

The Supreme Court's decision in this complex case was against Scott. Chief Justice **Roger B. Taney** wrote that African Americans were not citizens, and only citizens could sue in federal court. He said that living in free territory did not make Scott free. Lastly, the Fifth Amendment says no one can lose property without due process of law. Since slaves were property, Congress could not stop people from taking slaves into federal territory.

Many antislavery voices rose against the decision. This included the voice of an Illinois lawyer named **Abraham Lincoln**.

Underline the three decisions the Supreme Court made in the *Dred Scott* case.

LINCOLN-DOUGLAS DEBATES

In 1858 Abraham Lincoln ran for a U.S. Senate seat as the Republican candidate. His opponent was Democrat Stephen Douglas, who was up for reelection. During the campaign, the two men met several times for the **Lincoln-Douglas debates.** In the debates, Lincoln was careful not to talk about slavery in the existing slave states. Instead, he claimed the Democrats were trying to spread slavery across the nation.

During the second debate, Lincoln questioned Douglas about popular sovereignty. He wondered whether that belief went against the *Dred Scott* decision. In other words, how could the people ban what the Supreme Court allowed? Douglas restated his belief in popular sovereignty. His response is remembered as the **Freeport Doctrine**.

Why do you believe Lincoln would not talk about slavery in the existing slave states?

____

____

____

Why did Lincoln question Douglas's belief in popular sovereignty?

____

____

____

CHALLENGE ACTIVITY

Critical Thinking: Summarize Write a paragraph summarizing the impact of the Fifth Amendment on the Supreme Court's ruling in the *Dred Scott* case.

DIRECTIONS Write two adjectives or descriptive phrases that describe the term.

1. Abraham Lincoln ______________________

____

2. Dred Scott ______________________

____

3. *Dred Scott* decision ______________________

____

____

4. Freeport Doctrine ______________________

____

5. James Buchanan ______________________

____

6. John C. Frémont ______________________

____

7. Lincoln-Douglas debates ______________________

____

____

8. Republican Party ______________________

____

9. Roger B. Taney ______________________

____

10. Stephen Douglas ______________________

____

Name ______________________ Class ________________ Date __________

Lesson 4

MAIN IDEAS

1. John Brown's raid on Harpers Ferry intensified the disagreement between free states and slave states.
2. The outcome of the election of 1860 divided the United States.
3. The dispute over slavery led the South to secede.

Key Terms and People

John Brown's raid Brown's attack on the Harpers Ferry arsenal, which began on October 16, 1859

John C. Breckinridge pro-slavery candidate nominated by southern Democrats for the 1860 presidential election

Constitutional Union Party new political party that concentrated on constitutional principles

John Bell candidate nominated for the 1860 election by the Constitutional Union Party

Confederate States of America (the Confederacy) the country formed by seceding southern states

Jefferson Davis the Confederacy's first president

John J. Crittenden Kentucky senator who proposed a compromise to try to stop southern secession and a civil war

Lesson Summary

RAID ON HARPERS FERRY

John Brown was an abolitionist. He decided to use violence to try to stop slavery. He planned to lead an attack on the arsenal at Harpers Ferry, Virginia.

John Brown's raid began on October 16, 1859. Although he succeeded in taking the arsenal, federal troops overwhelmed him and his small band. They killed some of Brown's followers and captured others, including Brown himself. Brown was charged and found guilty of treason. On December 2, 1859, he was hanged for his crimes.

What did John Brown want to accomplish?

____

____

Many northerners agreed with Brown's anti-slavery beliefs, but they did not agree with his violent methods. Southerners worried that Brown's raid was the start of more attacks on the South.

Why do you think John Brown's raid scared southerners?

____

____

ELECTION OF 1860

The country was torn as the 1860 presidential election approached. The Democrats proposed two candidates—the North's Stephen Douglas and the South's **John C. Breckinridge**. In addition, the new **Constitutional Union Party** nominated **John Bell**. Abraham Lincoln ran on the Republican ticket.

Lincoln won the election, but he did not carry a southern state in his win. This angered southerners, who worried that they had lost their political power.

Underline the names of the presidential candidates who ran for election in 1860.

THE SOUTH SECEDES

Southern states responded to Lincoln's election with secession. These states joined together into a new country—the **Confederate States of America**. They elected Mississippian **Jefferson Davis** as their first president. In this country, slavery was legal.

What event led southern states to secede from the United States of America?

____

Lincoln argued that southern states could not secede from the Union. It seemed that even compromises, like one proposed by Kentucky Senator **John J. Crittenden**, would not mend this tear in the national fabric. President-elect Lincoln declared there could be no compromise where slavery was concerned. He also announced that the federal property in southern lands remained part of the United States.

CHALLENGE ACTIVITY

Critical Thinking: Analyze Write a paragraph explaining why the Democrats ran two candidates in the 1860 presidential election and the affect that had on the South's secession.

DIRECTIONS Write a word or phrase that means the opposite of the term given.

1. Confederate States of America ____

____

2. secession ____

____

DIRECTIONS Read each sentence and fill in the blank with the word in the word pair that best completes the sentence.

3. ______________________ was an attack on the arsenal at Harpers Ferry, Virginia, in 1859. (secession/John Brown's raid)
4. During the election of 1860, a new political party emerged called the ______________________. (Constitutional Union Party/Confederate States of America)
5. ______________________ was chosen as the Constitutional Union Party's candidate for president. (John J. Crittenden/John Bell)
6. ______________________ was elected president of the ______________________. (John J. Crittenden/Jefferson Davis); (Constitutional Union Party/Confederate States of America)
7. Senator ______________________ from Kentucky proposed a series of constitutional amendments he hoped would satisfy the South and save the Union. (John J. Crittenden/John Bell)
8. Abolitionist John Brown was executed for his part in the raid on ______________________. (Harpers Ferry/Confederate States of America)

Lesson 1

MAIN IDEAS

1. Following the outbreak of war at Fort Sumter, Americans chose sides.
2. The Union and the Confederacy prepared for war.

Key Terms and People

Fort Sumter federal post in Charleston, South Carolina, that surrendered to the Confederacy; marked the beginning of the Civil War

border states four slave states—Delaware, Kentucky, Maryland, and Missouri—that bordered the North and did not join the Confederacy

Winfield Scott Union general with a two-part strategy for defeating the Confederacy

cotton diplomacy Confederate plan to enlist Britain's aid in return for continued cotton shipments

Lesson Summary

AMERICANS CHOOSE SIDES

After being elected in 1860, Abraham Lincoln took office as seven southern states left the Union. He promised he would not end slavery where it existed. However, he also promised to preserve the Union.

How did the South react to Lincoln's election to the presidency?

____

____

Confederate officials already were taking control of federal mints, arsenals, and forts. Fighting finally broke out at **Fort Sumter**, a federal fort in the Confederate state of South Carolina. Federal troops refused to surrender to the Confederacy. Within two days, Fort Sumter fell. Lincoln called for 75,000 militiamen to put down the South's rebellion.

How did Lincoln respond to the surrender of Fort Sumter?

____

____

After Lincoln called for troops, all the states had to choose a side. Four more slave states joined the Confederacy. Four **border states**—slave states that bordered the North—decided to stay in the Union. In addition, western Virginia broke off from Confederate Virginia to stay in the Union.

Union general **Winfield Scott** had a two-part strategy to conquer the South. First, he would destroy the South's economy with a naval blockade of southern ports. Second, Scott would gain control of the Mississippi River, which would help divide the South.

The Confederacy had its own plan of attack. Part of that plan involved **cotton diplomacy**—the hope that Britain would support the Confederacy because it needed Confederate cotton. This strategy did not work because Britain had large stores of cotton and got more from India and Egypt.

Why didn't cotton diplomacy work?

____

____

PREPARING FOR WAR

Neither side was prepared for the war to come. However, many citizens—northern and southern— were eager to help. Thousands upon thousands of young men answered the call to arms and volunteered to serve in both armies.

Civilians, too, volunteered to help. They raised money to aid soldiers and their families. They staffed and supplied emergency hospitals. In the Union alone, about 3,000 women served as army nurses.

In what ways did civilians help the war effort?

____

____

____

Once the thousands of farmers, teachers, laborers, and others joined the armies, they had to be trained to become soldiers. They spent long days drilling and practicing with their guns and bayonets. As a result, many young soldiers were ready to fight.

CHALLENGE ACTIVITY

Critical Thinking: Design Write an advertisement encouraging people to support the soldiers by coming to a fundraising event.

Abraham Lincoln	cotton diplomacy	Winfield Scott
border states	Fort Sumter	

DIRECTIONS Use the five vocabulary words from the word list to write a summary of what you learned in the lesson.

____

____

____

____

____

____

____

____

____

____

____

DIRECTIONS Read each sentence and fill in the blank with the word in the word pair that best completes the sentence.

1. The Civil War began in 1861 when Confederate troops began to fire on ___________________. (border states/Fort Sumter)
2. Union general ___________________ planned to destroy the South's economy with a naval blockade of southern ports. (Abraham Lincoln/ Winfield Scott)
3. The South tried to win foreign allies through ___________________. (border states/cotton diplomacy)
4. In his inaugural address, ___________________ promised not to end slavery where it existed. (Abraham Lincoln/Winfield Scott)
5. Delaware, Kentucky, Maryland, and Missouri were ___________________ that did not join the Confederacy. (border states/cotton diplomacy)

Lesson 2

MAIN IDEAS

1. Union and Confederate forces fought for control of the war in Virginia.
2. The Battle of Antietam gave the North a slight advantage.
3. The Confederacy attempted to break the Union naval blockade.

Key Terms and People

Thomas "Stonewall" Jackson Confederate general who helped fight Union troops at the First Battle of Bull Run

First Battle of Bull Run battle near Manassas Junction, Virginia, in 1861

George B. McClellan general sent by President Lincoln to capture Richmond

Robert E. Lee Confederate general during many important battles of the Civil War

Seven Days' Battles series of battles that forced McClellan to retreat from near Richmond

Second Battle of Bull Run Confederate attack that helped push Union forces out of Virginia

Battle of Antietam battle in Maryland that resulted in Lee's retreat to Virginia

ironclads ships that were heavily armored with iron

Lesson Summary

WAR IN VIRGINIA

In July 1861 the Union and Confederate armies clashed near Manassas Junction, Virginia, along Bull Run Creek. At first the Union soldiers, under General Irvin McDowell, pushed back the left side of the Confederate line. Then southern troops, led by General **Thomas "Stonewall" Jackson**, fought back. With reinforcements arriving, the Confederate troops drove the Union army back. This conflict was called the **First Battle of Bull Run**. It showed that the war would not be an easy victory for the Union.

What did the First Battle of Bull Run show?

____

____

After the failed attempt to take Richmond, Lincoln tried again. This time he sent new commander General **George B. McClellan**. In the spring of 1862 McClellan led 100,000 soldiers, called the Army of the Potomac, on a slow march to Richmond.

Then, in June, General **Robert E. Lee** took command of the Confederate forces. On June 26 the two armies met in the **Seven Days' Battles**. These battles pushed McClellan away from Richmond. Lee saved Richmond and forced McClellan to retreat. Then during the **Second Battle of Bull Run**, Jackson's troops defeated another Union army before it could march directly on Richmond.

Underline all the Civil War battles identified on this page.

BATTLE OF ANTIETAM

A copy of Lee's battle strategy left behind led to the next major battle of the Civil War. The Union discovered the Confederates were going to attack Harpers Ferry. McClellan sent his troops to stop them. The two armies met along Antietam Creek in Maryland. The **Battle of Antietam** took place on September 17, 1862. It halted Lee's northward march. This battle was a success. However, it was the bloodiest single-day battle of the Civil War and of United States history. The Union suffered more than 12,000 casualties and the Confederates suffered more than 13,000 casualties.

BREAKING THE UNION'S BLOCKADE

Despite the distance it had to control, the Union blockade of southern ports was very effective. It reduced the number of ships entering southern ports from 6,000 to 800 per year. Both sides had the innovation of **ironclads**. However, the Union continued the blockade unbroken.

Underline the sentence that supports the statement that the Union blockade of southern ports was very effective.

CHALLENGE ACTIVITY

Critical Thinking: Explain How was a mistake responsible for the Battle of Antietam?

Battle of Antietam	ironclads	Seven Days' Battles
First Battle of Bull Run	Robert E. Lee	Thomas "Stonewall" Jackson
George B. McClellan	Second Battle of Bull Run	

DIRECTIONS Use five of the terms or names from the word bank to write a letter that relates to the lesson.

Dear ____

____

____

____

____

____

____

____

____

____

____

____

DIRECTIONS On the line provided before each statement, write **T** if a statement is true and **F** if a statement is false. If the statement is false, write the correct term on the line after each sentence that makes the sentence a true statement.

_____ 1. General <u>George B. McClellan</u> commanded the Confederate forces during the Seven Days' Battles. He saved Richmond and forced the Union army to retreat.

____

_____ 2. The <u>Battle of Antietam</u> was the bloodiest single-day battle of the Civil War, with a total of more than 25,000 casualties.

____

______ 3. The North's hopes of winning the war quickly and easily were crushed when the Union army was defeated at the Second Battle of Bull Run.

____

______ 4. General Thomas "Stonewall" Jackson led Confederate troops to victory during the First Battle of Bull Run.

____

Lesson 3

MAIN IDEAS

1. Union strategy in the West centered on control of the Mississippi River.
2. Confederate and Union troops struggled for dominance in the Far West.

Key Terms and People

Ulysses S. Grant Union general whose troops won several important battles on southern soil and in the western campaign

Battle of Shiloh battle in which Union troops gained greater control of the Mississippi River valley

David Farragut naval leader who helped the Union take control of New Orleans

Siege of Vicksburg six-week blockade of Vicksburg that starved the city into surrender

Lesson Summary

UNION STRATEGY IN THE WEST

In February 1862 General **Ulysses S. Grant** led a Union army into Tennessee. He was headed toward the Mississippi River. He wanted to capture outposts that would separate the eastern Confederacy from its western, food-supplying states. On the way Grant and his forces took both Fort Henry and Fort Donelson.

Why did the Union consider control of the Mississippi River critical?

Near Shiloh Church, Grant halted his troops to wait for more soldiers to arrive. Grant was aware of Confederate troops in the area. However, he was caught by surprise when they attacked on April 6. During the two-day **Battle of Shiloh**, each side lost and gained ground. Union reinforcements arrived. They helped push the Confederates into retreating. This win helped the Union control part of the Mississippi River valley.

How do you know that Fort Henry and Fort Donelson were Confederate forts?

To control the Mississippi River, the Union had to first deal with New Orleans. This was the South's largest city and the valuable port near the mouth of the Mississippi River. However, two forts guarded New Orleans from the south.

Union admiral **David Farragut** solved that problem. He disguised his boats and raced past the two forts in the darkness before dawn on April 24, 1862. Within days New Orleans fell to the Union troops. Farragut continued north, taking more cities, until he reached Vicksburg, Mississippi.

How was New Orleans captured?

____

____

____

Vicksburg was located on cliffs high above the Mississippi River. This allowed Confederate general John C. Pemberton to stop any attempt to attack the city. So, instead of trying to attack Vicksburg directly, General Grant cut the city off. He shelled it repeatedly. The **Siege of Vicksburg** lasted about six weeks before hunger forced the Confederates to surrender. The Mississippi River was now under Union control.

Why was Vicksburg difficult to capture?

____

____

____

Why did the Siege of Vicksburg succeed when attacks on Vicksburg had failed?

____

____

____

STRUGGLE FOR THE FAR WEST

The Confederates tried to take control of the southwest. So fighting also broke out there.

Defeats in Arizona and at Glorieta Pass stopped Confederates from taking lands in the West. Confederate-Union conflicts in Missouri also ended with a Confederate defeat. This was despite aid from the Cherokee. Attacks on Union forts and raids on towns forced the Union commanders to keep valuable troops stationed in the western states and territories.

CHALLENGE ACTIVITY

Critical Thinking: Analyze Write a paragraph analyzing why the Union wanted to control the West.

Battle of Shiloh	John C. Pemberton	Ulysses S. Grant
David Farragut	Siege of Vicksburg	

DIRECTIONS Answer each question by writing a sentence that contains at least one word from the word bank.

1. Which Union commander was the most important figure in the war in the West?

____

____

2. Who was the Union naval leader from Tennessee who captured New Orleans?

____

____

3. What is the name of the event where the Union army, under General Ulysses S. Grant, gained greater control of the Mississippi River?

____

____

4. Who was the Confederate general who attempted to defend the city of Vicksburg, Mississippi, from Union attack?

____

____

5. What event lasted about six weeks and ended when the Union captured Vicksburg, Mississippi?

____

____

Name ______________________ Class ______________ Date __________

Lesson 4

MAIN IDEAS

1. The Emancipation Proclamation freed slaves in Confederate states.
2. African Americans participated in the war in a variety of ways.
3. President Lincoln faced opposition to the war.
4. Life was difficult for soldiers and civilians alike.

Key Terms and People

emancipation the freeing of slaves

Emancipation Proclamation order to free Confederate slaves

contrabands escaped slaves

54th Massachusetts Infantry heroic unit of mostly free African American soldiers

Copperheads nickname for the Peace Democrats, a group who spoke out against the war

habeas corpus constitutional protection against unlawful imprisonment

Clara Barton army volunteer whose work was basis for the American Red Cross

Lesson Summary

EMANCIPATION PROCLAMATION

President Lincoln realized that one way to weaken the South was to free the slaves. **Emancipation** would free many slaves on which the South's economy relied. After the Battle of Antietam, Lincoln presented the **Emancipation Proclamation**. Despite the impossibility of enforcing it in Confederate-held states, the proclamation still had a distinct effect on the war.

What was the purpose of the Emancipation Proclamation?

AFRICAN AMERICANS PARTICIPATE IN THE WAR

In July 1862 Congress decided to allow African Americans to join the army as laborers. This decision included both free African Americans and **contrabands**, or escaped slaves. Within a year several African American units had formed. The most famous unit was the **54th Massachusetts**

How were contrabands different from other African Americans who joined the Union army?

Infantry. These troops helped attack South Carolina's Fort Wagner.

African American soldiers received less pay than white soldiers. They also faced greater danger. If captured by Confederates, they could be returned to slavery. In fact, Lincoln suggested these soldiers be rewarded by getting the right to vote.

GROWING OPPOSITION

Some midwesterners and northerners did not think the war was necessary. They called themselves Peace Democrats, but their enemies called them **Copperheads**, after the poisonous snake.

Lincoln saw Copperheads as a threat to the war effort. Because of this, he had Copperheads put in jail with no evidence and no trial. To do this, he ignored their right of **habeas corpus**. This is constitutional protection against unlawful imprisonment. Despite this and the northern draft, Lincoln won his second election in 1864.

What is habeas corpus?

____

____

LIFE FOR SOLDIERS AND CIVILIANS

For the soldier, both camp life and combat offered dangers. Poor camp conditions, including lack of medicine and painkillers, led to illness. This alone killed more men than battle did. Those wounded or captured in battle often met the same fate.

Those left behind took over the work of the men who went to war. In addition, many women also provided medical care for the soldiers. For example, volunteer **Clara Barton** collected medicine and supplies for the Union troops. Her work led to the forming of the organization that would become the American Red Cross.

How did women help the war effort?

____

____

____

CHALLENGE ACTIVITY

Critical Thinking: Contrast First, imagine you are a lawyer for the Peace Democrats. Write a paragraph explaining why the right of habeas corpus should not be ignored. Then imagine you are a lawyer for the federal government. Write a paragraph defending Lincoln's actions.

DIRECTIONS Read each sentence and fill in the blank with the word in the word pair that best completes the sentence.

1. The ________________________ called for all Confederate slaves to be freed. (habeas corpus/Emancipation Proclamation)
2. The ________________________ consisted mostly of free African Americans. (Emancipation Proclamation/54th Massachusetts Infantry)
3. ________________________ were a group of Northern Democrats who spoke out against the Civil War. (Contrabands/Copperheads)
4. ________________________ is the constitutional protection against unlawful imprisonment. (Habeas corpus/Emancipation)
5. ________________________ volunteered during the Civil War and organized the collection of medicine and supplies for delivery to Union troops on the battlefield. (Clara Barton/Copperheads)
6. The War Department gave ________________________, or escaped slaves, the right to join the Union army. (contrabands/Copperheads)
7. ________________________ is the freeing of slaves. (Habeas corpus/ Emancipation)
8. More soldiers died from ________________________. (poor camp conditons/ lack of medicine)
9. African American soldiers faced greater danger because they could be ________________________ if captured. (imprisoned/returned to slavery)
10. Although they faced greater danger, African American soldiers received ________________________. (the right to vote/less pay)

Name ______________________________ Class ____________________ Date ____________

MAIN IDEAS

1. The Union tried to divide the Confederate army at Fredericksburg, but the attempt failed.
2. The Battle of Gettysburg in 1863 was a major turning point in the war.
3. During 1864, Union campaigns in the East and South dealt crippling blows to the Confederacy.
4. Union troops forced the South to surrender in 1865, ending the Civil War.

Key Terms and People

Battle of Gettysburg three-day key battle that Confederates lost

George Pickett general who carried out Lee's orders to charge the Union line

Pickett's Charge disastrous attempt by Pickett's troops to storm Cemetery Ridge

Gettysburg Address speech in which Lincoln praised the bravery of Union soldiers and renewed his commitment to winning the war

Wilderness Campaign series of battles in which Grant tried to take Richmond

William Tecumseh Sherman Union general who cut a path of destruction across Georgia

total war strategy in which both civilian and military resources are destroyed

Appomattox Courthouse the place where Lee surrendered to Grant

Lesson Summary

FREDERICKSBURG AND CHANCELLORSVILLE

In late 1862 Confederate troops under the command of General Robert E. Lee won a battle at Fredericksburg, Virginia. In the spring of 1863 they again defeated Union troops at Chancellorsville.

BATTLE OF GETTYSBURG

Hoping a Confederate win on Union soil would break the Union's spirit, Lee headed into Union territory. The **Battle of Gettysburg**, which started July 1, 1863, was the consequence.

The first day, Lee's troops pushed Union general George G. Meade's soldiers back. The

Why did the Battle of Gettysburg start?

____

____

Union troops had to dig in on top of two hills outside the town. On the second day, Confederate troops tried to take the hill called Little Round Top but failed. On the third day, Lee ordered General **George Pickett** to lead a charge on Cemetery Ridge. **Pickett's Charge** was a disaster. Over half the Confederates were killed, and Lee retreated. Never again would his troops reach northern land. The Battle of Gettysburg was the turning point in the war.

How long did the Battle of Gettysburg last?

____

Who won the Battle of Gettysburg?

____

President Lincoln helped dedicate a new cemetery at Gettysburg. On November 19, 1863, he delivered the **Gettysburg Address**.

UNION CAMPAIGNS CRIPPLE THE CONFEDERACY

The **Wilderness Campaign** was a series of battles fought in Virginia around Richmond. Although he lost more men than Lee, Grant also had more reinforcements. As a result of the battles, Grant was winning the war. However, at Petersburg, Lee's defenses did not allow Grant to execute his attack and capture Richmond.

To assure his reelection, Lincoln needed a victory. General **William Tecumseh Sherman** provided it by capturing Atlanta, Georgia. This victory helped Lincoln get reelected in a landslide.

How did General William Sherman help President Lincoln get reelected?

____

____

____

Sherman did not stop at Atlanta. He ordered his troops to cut a path of destruction through Georgia, practicing **total war** all the way to the ocean.

THE SOUTH SURRENDERS

On April 9, 1865, at **Appomattox Courthouse**, Lee officially surrendered to Grant. The long, bloody war was over, but the question of how the United States could be united again remained.

In what year did the Civil War end?

____

CHALLENGE ACTIVITY

Critical Thinking: Sequence Use dates and events in this lesson to make a timeline of the Civil War.

Appomattox Courthouse	George Pickett	total war
Battle of Gettysburg	Gettysburg Address	Wilderness Campaign
George G. Meade	Pickett's Charge	William Tecumseh Sherman

DIRECTIONS On the line provided before each statement, write **T** if a statement is true and **F** if a statement is false. If the statement is false, write the correct term on the line after each sentence that makes the sentence a true statement.

______ 1. The <u>Battle of Gettysburg</u> was a turning point in the Civil War and made northerners believe the war could be won.

____

______ 2. The Battle of Gettysburg began when Confederate soldiers raided the city of Gettysburg and clashed with Union cavalry led by General <u>George G. Meade</u>.

____

______ 3. <u>William Tecumseh Sherman</u> carried out General Lee's order to attack the Union's line during the Battle of Gettysburg.

____

______ 4. Over half of the Confederate troops were killed in <u>total war</u>, which was a disastrous attack on Union forces at Cemetery Ridge during the Battle of Gettysburg.

____

______ 5. The Wilderness Campaign, given at the dedication of the cemetery at the Gettysburg battlefield, was a short but moving speech, and is one of the most famous speeches in American history.

____

______ 6. William Tecumseh Sherman carried out a campaign, known as total war, to destroy southern railroads and industries to ruin the South's economy and its ability to fight.

____

Name ______________________ Class ______________ Date __________

Reconstruction

Lesson 1

MAIN IDEAS

1. President Lincoln and Congress differed in their views as Reconstruction began.
2. The end of the Civil War meant freedom for African Americans in the South.
3. President Johnson's plan began the process of Reconstruction.

Key Terms and People

Reconstruction the process of readmitting the former Confederate states to the Union following the end of the Civil War

Ten Percent Plan Lincoln's Reconstruction plan, which required that 10 percent of voters in a state pledge loyalty to the United States before that state could rejoin the Union

Thirteenth Amendment the amendment that made slavery illegal throughout the United States

Freedmen's Bureau an organization established by Congress to provide relief for freedpeople and certain poor people in the South

Andrew Johnson vice president who became president upon Lincoln's death

Lesson Summary

RECONSTRUCTION BEGINS

As soon as the Civil War ended, Reconstruction began. **Reconstruction** was a period of reuniting the nation and rebuilding the southern states. The former Confederate states were readmitted to the union during this time.

What was the purpose of Reconstruction?

____

____

President Lincoln proposed that southerners be offered amnesty, or an official pardon. Southerners had to swear an oath of loyalty to the United States and accept the ban on slavery. When 10 percent of the voters in any state took the oath, that state could be accepted back into the Union. This was called the **Ten Percent Plan**.

Some supported the Wade-Davis Bill instead. The Wade-Davis Bill required southerners to ban slavery. However, under this bill, most of the people of a state would have to take the pledge before the state could rejoin the Union. Also, only southerners who swore they had never supported the Confederacy could run for office. Lincoln refused to sign the bill.

FREEDOM FOR AFRICAN AMERICANS

In 1865 the **Thirteenth Amendment** to the Constitution officially outlawed slavery in the nation. Former slaves reacted to freedom in many ways. They legalized their marriages, searched for relatives who had been sold, took new last names, and moved to new places.

What part of the Constitution granted freedom to all slaves?

____

To help the South's poor and freedpeople, Congress created the **Freedmen's Bureau** in 1865. One of its roles was to build more schools. Some freedpeople also established their own schools. Although some southerners violently resisted the idea of educating African Americans, freedpeople of all ages attended classes.

Why would southerners oppose the education of African Americans?

____

____

____

PRESIDENT JOHNSON'S RECONSTRUCTION PLAN

On April 14, 1865, President Lincoln was shot while attending the theater. He died the next morning. Vice-President **Andrew Johnson** became the next president. Johnson's Reconstruction plan included a way to restructure southern state governments. States that followed the steps were to be readmitted to the Union.

Why did Congress refuse to accept the southern states back into the Union?

____

____

____

Most of the southern states followed Johnson's plan, but Congress refused to accept them back into the Union. Many of the elected representatives of the "new" states had been Confederate leaders. Clearly there were still problems to be solved.

CHALLENGE ACTIVITY

Critical Thinking: Explain You are a citizen from a southern state. Write a letter to Congress explaining why it is your right to choose your state's representatives.

Andrew Johnson	Reconstruction	Thirteenth Amendment
Freedmen's Bureau	Ten Percent Plan	

DIRECTIONS Read each sentence and choose the correct term from the word bank to replace the underlined phrase. Write the term in the space provided and then define the term in your own words.

1. The time of reuniting the nation and rebuilding the southern states without slavery was called Ten Percent Plan. ______________________

   Your definition: ______________________

   ____

2. The Thirteenth Amendment was established to provide relief for poor people, black and white, in the South. ______________________

   Your definition: ______________________

   ____

3. The Freedmen's Bureau was the vice-president sworn into office after President Lincoln was shot while attending the theater and later died.

   ____

   Your definition: ______________________

   ____

4. Lincoln offered southerners amnesty for all illegal acts supporting the rebellion under the Thirteenth Amendment. ______________________

   Your definition: ______________________

   ____

5. Slavery was made illegal throughout the United States under the Ten Percent Plan. ______________________

   Your definition: ______________________

   ____

Lesson 2

MAIN IDEAS

1. Black Codes led to opposition to President Johnson's plan for Reconstruction.
2. The Fourteenth Amendment ensured citizenship for African Americans.
3. Radical Republicans in Congress took charge of Reconstruction.
4. The Fifteenth Amendment gave African Americans the right to vote.

Key Terms and People

Black Codes southern laws that greatly limited the freedom of African Americans

Radical Republicans Republicans who wanted more federal control in Reconstruction

Civil Rights Act of 1866 act giving African Americans the same legal rights as whites

Fourteenth Amendment amendment guaranteeing citizens equal protection of laws

Reconstruction Acts laws passed to protect African American rights

impeachment process of bringing charges of wrongdoing against a public official

Fifteenth Amendment amendment giving African American men the right to vote

Lesson Summary

OPPOSITION TO PRESIDENT JOHNSON

Almost as soon as the southern states created new legislatures, those legislatures went to work passing **Black Codes**. The Black Codes were laws that greatly limited the freedom of African Americans. In fact, the codes created working conditions that resembled slavery for African Americans. Many African Americans organized to protest codes.

The Black Codes angered many Republicans who believed the South was returning to its old ways. The **Radical Republicans** wanted the federal government to step in. They wanted more federal

What were Black Codes?

____

____

____

Who believed President Johnson's Reconstruction plan was a failure?

____

____

control over Reconstruction to make sure southern leaders did not remain loyal to the old Confederate principles. One Radical Republican leader was Pennsylvania's Thaddeus Stevens. Stevens and others pushed for racial equality. They branded Johnson's Reconstruction plan a failure.

FOURTEENTH AMENDMENT

In 1866 Congress proposed a bill to give more power to the Freedmen's Bureau. President Johnson vetoed it. He believed Congress could not pass new laws until the South was represented in Congress.

Then Congress proposed the **Civil Rights Act of 1866**. It guaranteed African Americans the same legal rights as whites. Johnson vetoed this, too. Congress overrode the veto. It also proposed the Fourteenth Amendment to secure these protections.

Circle the verb that shows that President Johnson was against the Civil Rights Act of 1866.

CONGRESS TAKES CONTROL OF RECONSTRUCTION

After the 1866 elections, Republicans held a two-thirds majority in both the House and Senate. As a result, Congress passed several **Reconstruction Acts**. It also passed a law limiting the president's powers to remove cabinet members without Senate approval. When President Johnson broke that law by firing his secretary of war, Congress reacted by impeaching the president. The **impeachment** fell short by one vote. Johnson remained president, though he had little authority or influence.

Why was President Johnson impeached?

____

____

FIFTEENTH AMENDMENT

Republicans believed that African Americans would support the Reconstruction plan. To gain their votes, Republicans in Congress proposed the **Fifteenth Amendment**, which guaranteed

Which Americans gained the right to vote as a result of the Fifteenth Amendment?

____

____

African American men the right to vote. This amendment went into effect in 1870.

CHALLENGE ACTIVITY

Critical Thinking: Summarize Find the Constitution in your textbook and read the entire Fourteenth and Fifteenth Amendments. Write a sentence summarizing each amendment.

DIRECTIONS On the line provided before each statement, write **T** if a statement is true and **F** if a statement is false. If the statement is false, write the correct term on the line after each sentence that makes the sentence a true statement.

_____ 1. The Civil Rights Act of 1866 provided African Americans with the same legal rights as white Americans.

____

_____ 2. The Fifteenth Amendment gave all African American men throughout the United States the right to vote.

____

_____ 3. The Reconstruction Acts were laws that restricted the overall freedom of African Americans.

____

_____ 4. Thaddeus Stevens was a leader of the Radical Republicans, who wanted racial equality for all Americans, including newly freed ones.

____

_____ 5. The Black Codes were laws passed by the Republican-controlled Congress to protect the rights of African Americans.

____

_____ 6. The Radical Republicans wanted the South to change much more than it already had before returning to the Union.

____

_____ 7. The Fourteenth Amendment ensured citizenship for African Americans.

____

MAIN IDEAS

1. Reconstruction governments helped reform the South.
2. The Ku Klux Klan was organized as African Americans moved into positions of power.
3. As Reconstruction ended, the rights of African Americans were restricted.
4. Southern business leaders relied on industry to rebuild the South.

Key Terms and People

Hiram Revels first African American senator

Ku Klux Klan secret society that used violence to oppress African Americans

Enforcement Acts laws providing equal protection for all under the law

Compromise of 1877 agreement in which Democrats accepted Hayes's election to the presidency in exchange for removing federal troops from the South

poll tax special tax people had to pay before they could vote

segregation forced separation of whites and African Americans in public places

Jim Crow laws laws that enforced segregation

Plessy* v. *Ferguson Supreme Court ruling that upheld segregation

sharecropping system in which farm laborers kept, or shared, some of the crop

Lesson Summary

RECONSTRUCTION GOVERNMENTS

Southerners did not trust northern Republicans who had moved south. They thought the newcomers sought profit from Reconstruction. African Americans used their new right to vote to elect more than 600 African Americans. The first black senator was **Hiram Revels**.

Who was the first African American senator?

____

KU KLUX KLAN

In 1866 a group of southerners created the secret and violent **Ku Klux Klan**. Its targets were African Americans, Republicans, and public officials. The Klan spread throughout the South until the federal government passed the

Circle the groups of Americans that were targeted by the Ku Klux Klan.

Enforcement Acts. The **Enforcement Acts** made Klan activities illegal.

RECONSTRUCTION ENDS

The General Amnesty Act of 1872 allowed most former Confederates to serve in public office. Soon many Democratic ex-Confederates were elected. Republicans also lost power because of Grant's problem-plagued presidency and the Panic of 1873. In 1876 the Hayes-Tilden presidential race was so close, it took the **Compromise of 1877** to make sure Democrats would accept Hayes's election.

Why did southern Republicans lose power during the 1870s?

____

____

____

Southern Democrats, called Redeemers, worked to limit African American rights. The methods they used included **poll taxes**, legal **segregation**, and **Jim Crow laws**. They even got help from the Supreme Court, which ruled in ***Plessy* v. *Ferguson*** that segregation was legal.

African Americans found their rights restricted in other ways, too. Most African Americans could not afford to buy land, so many began **sharecropping**. Sharecropping is sharing a crop with landowners. Often only the landowner profited. Sharecroppers lived in debt.

REBUILDING SOUTHERN INDUSTRY

The South's economy depended on cotton profits, which went up and down. In the "New South" movement, southern leaders turned to industry to strengthen the economy. Mills and factories were built. The new industries thrived and helped the southern economy grow stronger.

How was the economy of the "Old South" different from the economy of the "New South"?

____

____

____

RECONSTRUCTION IN THE NORTH

The new right of African American men to vote inspired women to work for their own suffrage. Northern African Americans gained some additional freedoms as well.

CHALLENGE ACTIVITY

Critical Thinking: Explain Write a paragraph explaining how the General Amnesty Act eventually led to the Compromise of 1877.

DIRECTIONS Read each sentence and fill in the blank with the word in the word pair that best completes the sentence.

1. A special tax that people had to pay before they could vote was called ________________________. (a poll tax/Jim Crow laws)
2. ________________________ was a system in which the landowners provided the land, tools, and supplies and workers provided the labor. (Segregation/ Sharecropping)
3. In ________________________, the U.S. Supreme Court allowed segregation if "separate-but-equal" facilities were provided. (the Compromise of 1877/ *Plessy* v. *Ferguson*)
4. ________________________ was the first African American in the U.S. Senate. (Hiram Revels/James Alcorn)
5. The removal of remaining troops from the South, funding for internal improvements, and the appointment of a southern Democrat to the president's cabinet were part of the ________________________. (Jim Crow laws/Compromise of 1877)
6. The forced separation of whites and African Americans in public places is called ________________________. (segregation/Ku Klux Klan)
7. The ________________________ was a secret society that opposed civil rights for African Americans and used violence and terror against them. (Ku Klux Klan/Jim Crow laws)
8. ________________________ were approved in southern states in the 1880s and allowed southerners to legally discriminate against African Americans. (Jim Crow laws/Segregationists)